Themes and Perspectives in Indian Sociology

D.N. Dhanagare

RAWAT PUBLICATIONS
Jaipur • New Delhi • Bengaluru • Guwahati • Kolkata

ISBN 978-81-7033-198-8 (hardback)

Reprinted, 2023

Published by
Prem Rawat for **Rawat Publications**
Satyam Apts., Sector 3, Jawahar Nagar, Jaipur - 302 004 (India)
Phones: 0141 265 1748 / 265 7006
E-mail : info@rawatbooks.com
Website: rawatbooks.com

New Delhi Office
4858/24, Ansari Road, Daryaganj, New Delhi 110 002
Phone: 011-23263290

Also at *Bengaluru, Guwahati* and *Kolkata*

Printed at Nice Printing Press, New Delhi

To
Ti. Swa. Anna
and
Sou. Meenakshivahinee

Contents

Preface

This book is a collection of my essays published in different periodicals from 1980 to 1990. For granting me permission to reproduce them here, I am thankful to the following: (i) *Seminar*: The Monthly Symposium (New Delhi) No. 254 (October 1980), pp. 23-26 for the article on "Search for Identity"; (ii) Wiley Eastern/UNESCO Paris, for the article on "Sociology and Social Anthropology in India" published in *Sociology and Social Anthropology in Asia and the Pacific* (ed. Y. Atal), 1984, pp. 313-60; (iii) Allied Publishers, New Delhi for the article on "Prospects of an Integrated Approach to Social Reality", published in *Philosophical Theory and Social Reality* (ed. Ravinder Kumar), 1984, pp. 168-83; and the UGC, New Delhi, since an earlier version of this article had appeared in the *Journal of Higher Education*, Vol. 7, No. 1 (Moonson 1981), pp. 97-109; (iv) *Sociological Bulletin* (the journal of the Indian Sociological Society), Vol. 35, No. 1 (September 1986), pp. 33-54 for the article on "Kosambi, Dialectical Materialism and the Structure and Dynamics of Indian Society"; (v) *Social Scientist*, Vol. 16, No. 11 (November 1988), pp. 18- 37 for the article on "Subaltern Consciousness and Populism"; (vi) Sage Publishers (India) and the Indian Council of Social Science Research for the article on "Action Groups and Social Transformation in India", published in the *Indian Journal of Social Science*, Vol. 1, No. 4 (October-December, 1988), pp. 37-59; and (vii) *Indian Journal of Social Work* (Tata Institute of Social Sciences, Bombay), Vol. L1, No. 1 (January 1990), pp. 1-13 for the article on "Relevance of Sociology".

Quite a few friends and colleagues have either read one or more of these essays and offered me their comments and useful suggestions before these were published. They include Yogesh Atal, U.B. Bhoite, Meera Kosambi, Satish Saberwal, R.S. Sharma, Yogendra Singh and Romila Thapar. While their inputs have helped me a great deal, they are in no way responsible for the deficiencies readers may find in my essays. I am grateful to all of them.

This book is dedicated to my elder brother and my sister-in-law (Bhabijee). My brother—Prof. P.N. Dhanagare—who teaches English at a college in Amravati (Maharashtra) may not have enjoyed professional visibility that teachers based in postgraduate departments of Indian universities do; however, I have always found him up-to-date in readings and with refreshingly new ideas. His reflective mind and strict sense of discipline as well as meticulousness about details have contributed richly to my upbringing in the family, and to my training in later years when we both did our postgraduation from Nagpur University. Though an elder sibling, he treated me more as a friend and peer and subjected my writings to ruthless scrutiny whenever I consulted him. The dedication of this book is a token repayment of the debt I owe.

D.N. Dhanagare

Chapter one

Introduction

These essays, written by me since 1980, embody my reflections on the growth of sociology as an intellectual discipline in India. These are addressed not only to the sociology profession but also to social sciences in India in general. While attempting to trace the entire development of sociology, the essays also try to bring out the dominant themes and perspectives that were mirrored in the way the craft of sociology was put to use by professional practitioners. The essays critically review the conditions that account for shifts in sociological concerns as well as in the theoretical and methodological orientations of Indian sociologists from time to time.

Throughout the essays, the readers would find 'sociology in India' and 'Indian sociology' as two expressions used interchangeably. The latter, according to Louis Dumont(1970: 1-32), is that specialised branch which stands at the confluence of Indology and sociology and which he advocates as the right type of 'mix' prerequisite to the understanding of Indian society. However, this specificity of usage is not subscribed to in these essays. Quintessentially, the essays are about 'sociology in India', the way it came to be institutionalised as an academic discipline and the phases of creative tension and joy it has gone through. In this sense, this collection of essays could be seen as a study in the broad arena of 'history of ideas, and sociology of knowledge', though basically the essays are about the course of development of sociology (and also social anthropology to a certain extent) in India.

Apart from the ICSSR-Surveys of Research Trend Reports (1972-74 and 1985-86) on different social sciences in India, very few have attempted critical self-analysis. Sociology in India is undoubtedly one discipline which has raised and answered questions about its own development during the past three decades or so.

A systematic beginning of reviewing the development of sociology in India was made by T.K.N. Unithan, Yogendra Singh, Indra Deva and N.K. Singhi (1965) in the 1960s itself. Nearly a decade and a half later, Ramkrishna Mukherjee's (1980) *Sociology of Indian Sociology* was published , after it first appeared as an article in *Current Sociology*. Some eight years later, Yogendra Singh's important work on *Indian Sociology*(1986) was published synchronising with the 11th World Congress of Sociology held at New Delhi in August 1986. At that time, another volume *Indian Sociology* was edited and published jointly by T.K. Oommen and Partha N. Mukherjee (1986). The works by Ramkrishna Mukherjee and Yogendra Singh were comprehensive review-essays, commissioned by the International Sociological Association. Both provide us with an excellent framework for analysing the trends in Indian sociology over the years. In my essays, I have benefited from both of these scholarly works. The volume edited by Oommen and Mukherjee contains articles written by eminent scholars but most of these articles were written before 1980 though their relevance to a critical appraisal of the development of sociology in India cannot be denied even today.

The essays in this volume, in contrast, were written by me alone over the decade 1980-1990. Any claim to perfect thematic unity among these essays would imply an attempt to overlook the diversity of themes and issues they deal with. Some overlapping is unavoidable since the essays were written at different times and for different purposes. As the author himself is part of the sociology profession in India, the volume in a sense presents an insider's view of sociology in India. In a way, the essays could therefore be seen as a self-portrayal of my own intellectual evolution, predilections and perhaps a few biases.

While tracing the development of any social science discipline—its themes and perspectives, whether recurrent or changing, two concepts are of cardinal importance. The first is 'epistemology' which generally refers to the study of assumptions about how to know the social reality and comprehend it.The second is, of course, 'methodology' by which we mean the study of techniques, approaches and practices used from time to time by professionals in the research process. The articles in this volume represent the current state of literature and emerging concerns in both these areas of sociology scholarship in India across a variety of fields as I viewed them in the 1980s.

Without appearing to be unduly modest, I must say that my status in the Indian sociology profession has been that of an 'outsider within', if I may use that expression. Not being a product of either the Lucknow School, the Bombay School or the Delhi School, which were the leading centres of training in sociology in the late 1950s when I studied, offered me a unique advantage. Neither was I under any pressure to conform to any specific line of sociological inquiry nor had I any inhibitions about using or not using specific research tools. Subsequently, from 1970 to 1973, I got the opportunity to study at the University of Sussex and completed a work which belongs in the grey area between comparative sociology and social history. However, professionally I always identified myself with the community of sociologists though with a self-imposed marginal status. As Patricia Hill Collins (1991: 2-3) has put it, "such a status of an 'outsider within' is more likely to challenge the knowledge claims of 'insiders', to acknowledge discrepancy and identify anomalies involving omissions and commissions of facts. Because the insiders are too immersed in and identified with, the process of knowledge production, they are more likely to miss these anomalies". To that extent, my status as an 'outsider within' in Indian sociology offered me some latent advantage whereby I could detach and distance myself from the mainstream of the sociology profession without being totally alienated from it at the same time.

Has sociology in India come to a dead-end facing some kind of intellectual stagnation? The chart of its knowledge production, creativity and innovativeness fromthe 1960s through the 1980s was most strikingly impressive by any standards. The growth was not only quantitative but also qualitative. During the last few years, since I wrote the essay on the "Relevance of Sociology, " which is included in and placed at the end of this collection, it has somehow been difficult to overcome the uncanny feeling that intellectual creativity in social sciences in general, and in sociology in particular, is either stationary or is declining. I must, however, add a rider here that though some leading figures in the profession have been able to maintain their individual creativity and even heighten it to some extent, centres or schools of sociological study appear to be losing their collective vitality and urge for knowledge production except that which falls off into mediocrity.

Randall Collins, in a recent essay (1992: 73-96) has also commented on intellectual stagnation in Western Sociology. He argues that periods of creativity were often followed by periods of creative slackness in history and has attributed this intellectual decline to three factors or conditions: (i) the centres of higher learning and research become the most decadent places due to 'loss of their cultural capital', so their own intellectual culture comes to a deadhalt. Although chairs and other organisational infrastructures remain as skeletons, most teachers, pupils and researchers get preoccupied with factional rivalries and horse-trading rather than with sustained academic work; (ii) ideas cease to flourish in academia because of the 'dominance of the classics'. This means that ideas of the great thinkers over-shadow those of their successors. This inhibits growth of new ideas; and (iii) 'technical refinement' involving conceptual development and technical innovation can also act as a double-edged weapon. Whereas, on one hand , such a refinement sharpens knowledge production, on the other, it can also develop technological obsessions among practising scientists. Such a technical refinement often runs the risk of becoming an end in itself. Paradoxically, it brings 'development' in one sense, but is more often likely to lead to freezing of ideas and to intellectual stagnation.

In referring to Collins' essay somewhat extensively in this introduction, my purpose is to share my concerns and impressions about the state of sociology in India as I think it is time that the organised profession ponders over this question of intellectual stagnation and sterility. If the craft has indeed landed into such an impasse, then it is necessary that efforts are made to find a way out as the profession prepares to face the challenges facing Indian society at the turn of the century and while entering the third millennium. Of course, the essays in this collection do not address directly this question of declining creativity and intellectual stagnation. In my last essay on the "Relevance of Sociology", the question has been dealt with only obliquely where I suggest that a seemingly flourishing academic discipline can render itself irrelevant if it does not address itself to existential problems of society. My personal preference is, however, for letting one's own voice of conscience determine the relevance of academic work. The question still remains, whether unorchestrated voices of conscience can unwittingly breed what Collins has termed as 'stagnation'. It should be helpful if this question is debated on in the profession more seriously and urgently.

In an introduction of this kind, it is customary to introduce the essays included in such a collection. However, instead of giving summaries of the contents of each article, it would be worthwhile to provide readers with some background details of the context in which these were written , and of those friends and colleagues who have helped me in clarifying my ideas and sharpening my argument, the if at all I have succeeded in making any.

The essay on "Search of Identity" was written on an invitation from late Romesh Thaper to contribute to *Seminar's* monthly symposium on "Understanding Society". I had never written for *Seminar* earlier and perhaps the invitation was a kind of an affectionate follow-up on my meeting him at a seminar held in Pune a little before he thought of planning the symposium. The special issue of the *Seminar* was due in October 1980 and because of an unfortunate tragedy in the family I had missed the deadline by almost two months. Though written in great haste, it was transformed into a readable manuscript by Satish Saberwal who edited that particular issue.

The second article is in the nature of a status-report on sociology and social anthropology in India. It was commissioned by the UNESCO Regional Unit for Human and Social Sciences in Bangkok which was keen on bringing out profiles of sociology in ten different countries of the South Asia and the Pacific regions. Dr. Yogesh Atal, Regional Adviser, UNESCO, helped me in defining the scope of the assignment and made certain stylistic changes in the essay. But for the UNESCO offering me this important assignment, I would not have written this article.

What appears in this volume as the essay, "Towards an Integrated Approach to Social Reality," is the reincarnation of a paper I first presented on "Interdisciplinary Approach to Social Reality in Social Sciences" at a seminar on the same theme at the Tilak Maharashtra Vidyapeeth in Pune. Subsequently, when Prof. Ravinder Kumar invited me to participate in a national seminar he organised at the Nehru Memorial Museum and Library in New Delhi on "Philosophical Theory and Social Reality" sometime in 1982, it gave me an opportunity to present a revised version of the same paper. If I recall correctly, my paper evoked a lot of criticism. Some useful suggestions also came from very senior social scientists including Prof. Ramkrishna Mukherjee, Prof. A.K. Saran and Prof. Rajni Kothari. I have richly benefited from their criticism, though I am not sure whether I was able to improve while producing a final revised version that appeared in a volume edited by Prof. Ravinder Kumar.

The next essay on Kosambi's "dialectical materialism" first emerged in the form of my lecture notes. While teaching a course on "Indian Society" as a part of the M.A. Sociology syllabus at Poona University , we often made cursory references to "application of dialectical method in understanding the structure and dynamics of Indian society" and cited D.D. Kosambi and his celebrated works as an example without getting deeper into the rigour of his analysis. An opportunity to discuss this theme comprehensively came at the time of the 11th World Congress of Sociology held in New Delhi in 1986. At the Congress, a special session on "Dialectical Sociology" was organised by the Soviet Sociological Society. After my presentation, Prof. Anaur Abdel

Mulleck commented on it and gave me the benefit of his learned advice.

The essay on "Subaltern Consciousness and Populism" has an equally fascinating origin. A part of this article was first drafted in the form of a review article on Ranajit Guha's (1983) seminal work, which was a precursor of what later developed into a major theoretical, almost paradigmatic orientation in "the other history" known as the "subaltern studies" approach (Guha ed. 1982-87). The series on subaltern studies was originally conceived in the summer of 1977 by Ranajit Guha. At this time, I happened to be in England and took the opportunity to interact with him, though only for a week, at the Sussex University where I had a very fruitful and stimulating interaction with Ranajit Guha while I was writing my doctoral dissertation. I owed an intellectual debt to him and yet did not join the group that eventually shaped the contours of the 'subaltern' approach. My own reaction was that in turning the 'elite historiography' of a neo-colonialist or a neo-nationalist variety upside down, the proponents of the subaltern historiography are committing the other error of throwing the baby with the bath water and of sidelining even a meaningful class analysis. I found the corrective in the concept of 'populism' as an analytical framework, though I must confess that my own ideas on the application of this framework in the Indian context are still in the formative stage. The article on 'two approaches' was first written in May 1988 when I spent a month as Visiting Professor at the Department of Sociology, North-Eastern Hill University, Shillong. To present these ideas, two quick opportunities came my way. First, the North-East Regional Centre of ICSSR invited me to deliver a special lecture while I was there. Later the same year, the Indian Council of Historical Research, especially Prof. Irfan Habib, the then chairman invited me to join an ICHR's official delegation to participate in India-USSR Joint Seminar on "Peasants in History" held at Moscow in October 1988 , and allowed me to present the same paper.

The theme of the next essay happens to be "Action Groups and Social Transformation". Being interested in studying movements,

I was naturally drawn to a series of articles by Rajni Kothari, D.L. Sheth and Harsh Sethi on 'non-party political processes,' published in *Economic and Political Weekly* from 1984 onwards. This was in a way an intellectual response to the experiences of the Emergency (1975-77), the experiment of the Janata Government—a non-Congress alliance—and its failure (1977-80), and the return of Indira Gandhi to power in 1980. Their entire thrust in favour of grass-roots level mobilisation and people's initiatives as a developmental alternative appealed to my intellectual sensitivities and I wrote that paper for presentation at the International Congress of Anthropological and Ethnological Sciences, held at Zagreb in 1988. Its publication in three periodicals—*Indian Journal of Social Science, Man and Development* and *Lokayan Bulletin* —caused some embarrassment, though I humbly feel that it did succeed in drawing the attention of professional sociologists to the whole phenomena of the action groups that occupy spaces between organised politics and mass movements—sometimes serving as linkages between them but more often distancing themselves from both.

The last essay in this volume is about the "Relevance of Sociology," and what really are the criteria for evaluation of that relevance in the Indian context. Sometime in 1984, Yogendra Singh had written two serialised articles on a similar theme and these had appeared in a journal called *Relevant Sociology* (Editor: Dr. J.S. Gandhi). I thought these articles raised a number of substantive issues but had also missed some. They had stirred my mind and I was planning to write a comment on them. In the summer of 1987, the All India Sociological Conference held at Shillong had a session on "Relevance of Sociology," and the organisers asked me to prepare a working paper on this theme. I presented this paper there and received numerous comments and suggestions from those who attended the session.

The purpose of putting these essays in a book is to make them together available to all those interested in understanding and evaluating the cognitive structure of Indian sociology. In doing so, it is hoped that the thrust of the essays on synthesising the scientific outlook, a precondition of performing sociological tasks, with value-commitments of sociologists, would not be missed by the readers.

References

Collins, P.H., 1991, "Learning from the Outsider Within—the Sociological Significance of Block Feminist Thought", in Mary Margaret Fonow and Judith A. Cook (Eds.), *Beyond Methodology: Feminist Scholarship as Lived Research*, Indiana University Press, pp. 35-59

Collins, Randall, 1992, "On the Sociology of Intellectual Stagnation—the Late Twentieth Century in Perspective", *Theory, Culture and Society*, Vol. 9, pp. 73-96.

Dumont, L., 1970, *Homo Hierarchicus: The Caste System and its Implications*, London: Weidenfeld and Nicolson.

Guha, R., 1983, *Elementary Aspects of Peasant Insurgency in Colonial India*, New Delhi: Oxford University Press.

——— (Ed.), 1982-87, *Subaltern Studies: Writings on South Asian History and Society*, Vols. I and V, New Delhi: Oxford University Press.

Indian Council of Social Science Research, 1972, 1974, *A Survey of Research in Sociology and Social Anthropology*, Vols. I-III, Bombay: Popular Prakashan.

———, 1985, 1986, *Survey of Research in Sociology and Social Anthropology 1969-1979*, Vols. I-III, New Delhi: Satvahan Publications.

Mukherjee, R., 1980, *Sociology of Indian Sociology*, Bombay: Allied.

Oommen, T.K. and Mukherjee, Partha N. (Eds.), 1986, *Indian Sociology: Reflections and Introspections*, Bombay: Popular Prakashan.

Singh, Y., 1986, *Indian Sociology: Social Conditioning and Emerging Trends*, New Delhi: Sage/Vistaar.

Unithan, T.K.N., Singh, Y., Deva, Indra and Singhi, N.K. (Eds.), 1965, *For a Sociology of India*, New Delhi: Prentice Hall of India.

Chapter two

Search for identity

Like an accomplished *sadhu* who is hesitant to disclose his family origins and antecedents, professional sociologists are often wary of facing squarely the refractory question: what is sociology? Not that this question has precise answers on which there can be unanimity. In fact, most leading sociologists in India, as elsewhere, would feel embarrassed if confronted with such an intriguing and equally vexing question. I am reminded of a historic moment when a non-professional came to the rescue of professional sociologists who have always been in search of a proper self-definition and identity. At the Ninth World Congress of Sociology, held at the picturesque campus of the University of Uppsala in Sweden in August 1978, the mayoress of Uppsala, while welcoming the delegates, commented on the printed programme of sessions of various panels, working groups, research committees and the like. The programme itself ran into over 300 pages.[1] 'Its contents reveal that sociology is everything and everything is sociology', she observed to everyone's delight.

However innocuous the remark may sound to those who look to sociology more with a sense of vanity than with social commitment, it truly epitomizes the present impasse, identity crisis and the lack of direction in the field of sociology in India as elsewhere.

The nature of such a crisis in western sociology has been under discussion and diagnosis for some time now. Partly the crisis in sociology simply portrays 'a modern society in which identity itself is uncertain and in flux'.[2] In such a society its members continually attempt, not always successfully, to adapt to their everchanging roles that are often mutually inconsistent and conflicting.

Hence, any attempt towards 'understanding men in society'

(as sociology is sometimes defined) would not be free from contradictions inherent in the very object of understanding. These conflicts and contradictions in the social matrix get reflected in the idiom of social theory which, says Alvin Gouldner, is in a state of utter crisis.[3] The crisis characterizes all academic sociology and more so the whole spectrum of sociological theories ranging from functionalism to different varieties of Marxism.

To what extent did sociology in India experience the vibrations of this crisis; and how has the discipline or the organized profession responded to it? In India the development of sociology as an academic discipline and its institutionalization in universities have followed a zig-zag course. In the pre-independence era, the colonial interests unmistakably shaped the initial attempts to understand Indian society—its cultural as well as structural angularities. That sociology and social anthropology appeared in Indian universities on this colonial backdrop[4] must be borne in mind constantly. Then only will it be possible to assess what sociology in India has been like, what strength or deficiencies it has revealed so far and what tasks are ahead for sociologists in India.

Initially, more dominant social science partners treated sociology as a 'residual category' and consequently it was relegated to a subordinate position in the organizational structures of universities. By sheer historical accidents sociology came to be tagged on to economics in some universities and to anthropology, politics or social work in others. Sociology's academic fate or fortune hinged partly on its perceived functional utility, and partly on how well-entrenched the 'big brothers' were in the local power structures of their universities. In my opinion, the image of sociology in India could rarely outgrow this initial rickety constitution despite sumptuous nourishment since the early 1950's.

Sociology in India initially emulated several models depending upon which disciplinary 'master' it has to serve under. It became necessary to adopt the conceptual apparatus, phraseology and even methodological equipment of those disciplines with whom sociology had to strike a symbiotic relationship in order to first survive and then to thrive. Its research interests sometimes centered around themes like 'socio-economic conditions of...' if it happened to be a part of an economics department. Numerous ethnic groups—castes, sub-castes, clans or tribes—figured predominantly in its concerns where sociology had to enter into wedlock with anthropology. When it had to grow under the shelter of 'social work', professional sociologists devoted themselves to studying the problems of the handicapped—physically or otherwise, of juvenile delinquents, of prostitutes and destitutes, and the most hackneyed 'worker-management problems' in industrial organizations.

Among the diverse ties of Indian sociologists, the last with 'social work' may have been the most damaging, for it encouraged sociologists to view contemporary social problems in terms not of social structure or process but of social pathology. 'Problems' were inherently bad, aberrations, 'dysfunctional to the system' and hence requiring 'eradication'.[5] It is noteworthy that the acceptance of such value-premises was far from conscious: these were quietly absorbed in universities and institutions where one found an academic home. The sociologist did not define his own roles: he received them for performance from his placement.

Being conditioned to be at the receiving end, Indian sociology could not come of age. Like an aged infant it failed to develop its own identity even after the 1950s when the discipline and the institutionalized profession witnessed phenomenal expansion. Noticeable during this expansion was a shift of concerns from the 'city' to the 'countryside', coinciding with the rise of 'community development'. But with that, Indian sociology got saddled with the stereotyped theme of 'the impact of community development on...', which came to dominate the research priorities of Indian sociology.

It was primarily the official patronage which enticed quite a few sociologists and social anthropologists to embrace this interest. Not that there was anything inherently wrong with this growing edge of the discipline. But then the State practically dictated research priorities and the policy concerns came to echo in sociology seminars and conferences. It can be surmised that at least some of the top professional sociologists in India espoused 'community development', perhaps angling for a share in the State's policy-formulation and thereby for extra-academic power within the State apparatus.

The parasitic, satellite existence of sociology has produced some side-effects. As status-seekers, Indian sociologists got used to accepting conceptual frameworks handed down to them, together with attendant sets of values, as given and not as a matter of critical evaluation. Consequently, there was very little creative involvement in social theory. There are, of course, notable exceptions (D.P. Mukerji, Ramkrishna Mukherjee, A.R. Desai, Y.B. Damle and Yogendra Singh, to mention a few) but their impact on Indian sociology was negligible. By and large the tendency was to use sociological theory ritually in empirical research, which really contributed very little to theory construction or even to the development of conceptual alternatives in the study of Indian social realities.

Since theoretical concerns did not figure very prominently in the practice of sociology in India, the kind of crisis that characterized western sociology, particularly in the realm of theory, did not produce any reverberations in Indian sociology at all. Basically, we find an abysmal lack of curiosity about anything very much, and that included the relevance of the theoretical advances in western social science for understanding Indian society. May be our social backgrounds and origins made us think that we did not need that kind of creative involvement in social theory for coping with the environment. Or it may be that the academic pecking order inhibited the breaking of ranks. The near-absence of theoretical concerns resulted in an inadequate understanding of society.

During the 1950s and 1960s, sociology on the Anglo-American and the European scenario was being swept by major transformations in ideas that came like the tidal waves of intellectual movements. Structural-functionalism underwent complete metamorphosis; different shades of structuralism, represented by Leach and Levi-Strauss, Althusser and Sartre were permeating the intellectual traditions in Europe and elsewhere; varieties of Marxism, existentialism and structuralism were being blended with one another; and a whole range of new developments within 'symbolic interactionism', the phenomenological school and in the Frankfurt School of Sociology were taking place.[6]

While these critical developments were reshaping western sociology, Indian sociologists were still debating whether 'sociology *for* India' was a more appropriate formulation than either 'sociology *in* India' or '*of* India'.[7] Their academic concerns were stagnant, and the profession wallowed complacently in studies of caste, tribe, village, marriage, family and kinship. However eminent an Indian sociologist might otherwise be, 'the sociology establishment' in India rarely considered him literate enough to be invited to seminars if he had not studied either 'kinship structure', 'caste' or at least a 'village'. The very narrowness of these interests obviated the need for theory which concerns general relationships seen apart from particular contexts; one is driven to theory when the contexts of enquiry are diversified. *Indian sociologists in some ways forestalled the need for theory by stereotyping the contexts of research.*

Like their ambivalence to theory, another striking feature of many Indian sociologists was their obsession for microcosmic empirical investigations of social settings. So great was that obsession that 'field-work' phase became a geographic metaphor and 'my village' became the Indian village. Whether it was Shamirpet or Rampura, Shivpur or Ramgarhi, these were either projected or perceived as quintessentially Indian villages.

The gap between the micro-setting (the object of direct observation) and the macro-setting of the pan-Indian society (for which abstractions and generalizations are made) was too wide to be filled by isolated, and often unrelated, empirical investigations on social microcosms. But the gap has not deterred some from composing grandiose profiles of macro-social processes in Indian society by using stray micro-level findings.[8] In fact, not only is there a wide gap between 'micro' and 'macro' but also sometimes the two may show contrary tendencies.

This is true not only in the Indian context but in any situation of multi-level complexity where it is impossible for a 'locality' to be a representative microcosm of the whole. Saberwal, for example, found noticeable social mobility among the scheduled castes in a Punjabi town but later confessed that the all-India situation did not really correspond to that rosy picture.[9]

Theoretical orientation was, however, not totally missing in Indian sociology. An overwhelming majority of Indian sociologists had found 'structural-functionalism' as an intellectually challenging as well as a satisfying framework. At a seminar held at the Agra University Institute of Social Sciences in the 1960s, most of the present-day stalwarts in Indian sociology acknowledged structural-functionalism as the most appropriate theoretical framework for understanding Indian society and social institutions.[10] Other perspectives—whether the Marxian, Weberian or Parsonian—were often rejected without even an acquaintance. Some isolated sociologists like late D.P. Mukerji and A.R. Desai, plough the lonely furrow of Marxian sociology[11] as Y.B. Damle and a few others did with the Parsonian framework.[12]

The purpose here is not either to undermine the importance of 'structural functionalism' or even to attempt a critique, but simply to draw attention to the peculiar development of sociology in India. With the acceptance of 'structural-functionalism' as an intellectual creed, sociologists tended to focus on the present structures of social relations and institutional arrangements as 'harmonic systems' and failed to highlight the conflicting forces and contradictions inherent in those systems.

This total immersion in the 'present' very subtly alienated us from history. Indian society and social institutions have had a long evolutionary history but most of the professional sociologists were over-committed to 'functionalism' as mentioned before. Their interest was confined to understanding only the present structures and functional interdependence among their parts. This resulted in the neglect of the socio-historical perspective which would have enriched our understanding of Indian society—its past and present problems and future prospects or directions of development.

Nothing could substantiate this point better than the confessions of an eminent Indian sociologist and social anthropologist:

> In course of time I became an enthusiastic convert to functionalism *a la* Radcliffe-Brown. I had the feeling that I had at last found a theoretical framework which was satisfactory but like all new converts I was fanatic. I suppressed my natural scepticism, one of my few real assets, to accept such dogmas as the irrelevance of history for sociological explanation, the unimportance of culture and the existence of universal laws.[13]

Although the lack of awareness of the relevance of history for sociological inquiries was characteristic of the pre-1970 phase of Indian sociology, some like Ramkrishna Mukherjee, A.R. Desai and a few others did use history fruitfully.[14] More recently, Yogendra Singh in his study of modernization,[15] Saberwal in his assessment of the colonial impact on urbanism and social inequalities,[16] Partha N. Mukherjee, Rajendra Singh and a number of younger sociologists, who have of late taken to studies on protest movements and revolts of the peasants, workers and the weaker sections in India have also rediscovered the inherent value of the classical tradition of comparative history for sociological analysis.[17]

I am not taking a historicist position. My argument is that history, although not sufficient, is certainly necessary to deepen our understanding of social realities in India today. My advocacy is in favour of 'using' history, and not 'doing' it. Sociologists, in my view, need to learn to read between the lines of historical writings. The better historians, too, are acutely interested in questions of causality, generalization, etc., but they also accept the demands of readability and, therefore, they build these questions into their narrative unobtrusively. Tracing the historical origins and process of development of social phenomena enriches our understanding in ways that the raw empiricism of facts-collection through standardized questionnaires or interview-schedules may miss altogether. I have found particularly the medieval and colonial periods of Indian history very relevant for studying the agrarian social structure, class relations and various facets of rural transformation as well as of peasant resistance in India.[18]

Not only that, using history sensitizes sociologists to their own specific socio-cultural milieu, and they get better equipped to ask sociologically more meaningful and purposeful questions. Fortunately, we have excellent and well-maintained source-material in India, thanks to the colonial bureaucracy—particularly in the field of land revenue administration. If at least a small part of one's field-work time is spent in a first-hand perusal of such historical material on land settlements, land alienation and land litigations, it would be immensely rewarding for sociologists interested in locating the roots of social inequalities in India, the institutionalization of different forms of oppression and exploitation, and above all in understanding why the oppressed rebel under certain social conditions.

Certainly, these academic interests could not possibly be 'value-free' in the sense the Weberian methodological dictum is generally understood. A more purposeful social science has to be 'value-based' which does not mean that it has to forsake its basic commitment to all canons of objectivity. Mere understanding of society and social phenomena is not enough; it is necessary to change them in 'desired directions'. Sociologists in India can richly contribute to social criticism, at least to the debate on 'what are those desired directions—in terms of both ends and means'. As members of society they owe this much debt. To repay it, Indian sociology must search for better allies in social science disciplines.

In other words, sociology must grow more as 'social criticism'[19] if it has to justify its existence particularly in a developing society like ours. To imagine that this task of social criticism goes well only with highly literate societies where ideas are being extensively discussed, and that in India no one cares to read criticism, is to indulge in cynicism. The call is for criticism anchored in social commitment, criticism that is socially relevant and is a response to our fast changing environment.

If these tasks are to be fulfilled, Indian sociology must reorient itself; it should be more concerned with social theory, be better rooted in history, must attempt constantly to balance between the 'micro' and 'macro' analytical perspectives, be honest enough to admit its value-premises and value-commitments, and must turn to the 'masses' rather than to elites. We have overdone 'caste' so far; let us explore the 'class' underpinnings of what are seemingly 'caste-relations, caste-conflicts and caste-atrocities'.[20] Let the classical sociological traditions—Comte, Marx, Weber, Durkheim and Pareto—not be forgotten. But it will not suffice to swear only by them. To build on those foundations without losing sight of the historical specificity of the Indian society is the crying need of our time.

Vast sections of the underprivileged in the Indian society, who have failed to make it through the 'mobility' route, are going to resort to the alternative 'mobilization' route to social transformation. What are the prospects of 'mobilization', where is it likely to lead, and would social scientists, including sociologists, like to be just silent, indifferent spectators of the transformation process or would they like to contribute to it in some measure? These are some of the questions the sociology profession as a whole must address itself to, sooner than later.

Notes and references

1. For details see: 9th World Congress of Sociology. *Programme Paths of Social Development*, Uppsala University, Sweden, August 14-19, 1978.
2. P.L. Berger, *Invitation of Sociology: A Humanistic Perspective.* New York: Anchor, 1963, pp. 48-49.
3. A.W. Gouldner, *The Coming Crisis of Western Sociology.* New York: Basic Books, Inc., 1970, particularly preface, also pp. 341-410.
4. For the colonial origins of Indian sociology and social anthropology see: K. Gough, 'Anthropology: Child of Imperialism', *Monthly Review*, 19 (11), 1966, pp. 12-27; also by her, *Towards an Anthropology*, London: Monthly Review Press, 1975.
5. This remark by C. Wright Mills on the American sociology in the 1940s and 1950s applies to the experience of Indian sociology as well. See: C. Wright Mills, *Power, Politics and People.* New York: Ballantine Books, 1962, pp. 525-552.

6. John Rex (Ed.), *Approaches to Sociology: An Introduction to Major Trends in British Sociology.* London: Routledge & Kegan Paul, 1974.
7. For example, see: *Contributions to Indian Sociology* (old series), No. I (1957), pp. 7-41; No. III (1959), pp. 88-101; and No. IV (1960), pp. 82-89; also see T.K.N. Unnithan, Y. Singh, N.K. Singhi and I. Dev (eds.), *Sociology for India.* New Delhi: Prentice-Hall of India, 1967.
8. See, for example, M.N. Srinivas, *Social Change in Modern India.* Bombay: Allied Publisher, 1966.
9. S. Saberwal, 'Sociologistists and Inequality in India: The Historical Contest'. *Economic and Political Weekly,* 14 (1079), pp. 243-54.
10. See: *Sociology in India* (*Seminar*, 10-15 December, 1964 Report), Institute of Social Sciences, Agra University, Agra, 1965.
11. D.P. Mukerji, *Diversities.* New Delhi: People's Publishing House, 1958; A.R. Desai, *Social Background of Indian Nationalism,* Bombay: Popular, 1976.
12. Y.B. Damle, 'For a Theory of Indian Sociology', in *Sociology in India* (seminar report), *op. cit.*, pp. 32-52.
13. M.N. Srinivas, 'Itineraries of an Indian Social Antropologist'. *International Social Science Journal,* XXV, 1-2 (1973), p. 141.
14. Ramkrishna Mukherjee, *The Dynamics of Rural Society.* Berlin: Akademic Verlag, 1957; also by him, *The Rise and Fall of the East India Company.* Berlin: Verlag der Wissenschafter, 1958; and A.R. Desai, *op. cit.*, 1976.
15. Y. Singh, *Modernization of Indian Tradition (A Systemic Study of Social Change).* Delhi: Thomson, 1973.
16. S. Saberwal, 'Indian Urbanism: A Socio-Historical Perspective'. *Contributions to Indian Sociology* (N.S.) 11 (1977), pp. 1-19; also by him, 'Inequality in Colonial India'. *Contributions to Indian Sociology* (N.S.), 13 (No. 2), 1979, pp. 241-64.
17. Some of these studies have been reported in M.S.A. Rao (ed.), *Social Movements in India,* Vols. I-II. Delhi: Manohar, 1978-79 and also in A.R. Desai (Ed.), *Peasant Struggles in India.* Bombay: Oxford University Press, 1979.
18. See my book: *Peasant Revolts in India,* c-1920-1950 (in press).
19. I have used the expression 'sociology as social criticism' in the sense Norman Birnbaum and Tom Bottomore have used it. See: N. Birnbaum, *Towards a Critical Sociology.* New York: Oxford University Press, 1971; T. Bottomore, Critics of Society. London: George Allen and Unwin, 1969, pp. 9-19; also by him, *Sociology as Social*

Criticism. New York: Pantheon Books, 1974, pp. 90-94.

20. Andre Beteille has significantly contributed to the studies of these conflicts. See his, 'Agraian Unrest in Tanjore', *The Times of India*, 20 September, 1969. 'Peasant Associations and the Agrarian Class Structure', *Contributions to Indian Sociology* (N.S.) 4 (1970) and also *Studies in Agrarian Social Structure*. New Delhi: Oxford University Press, 1974. Also A. Ghosh, 'Caste Collisions', *Seminar*, June 1980.

Chapter three

Sociology and social anthropology in India

The development of social sciences, in general, corresponds with the development of modern industrial capitalism in Europe. The relationship between the two is far from accidental or coincidental. Although in the history of ideas it may be possible to find certain thought-systems and ways of interpreting or understanding society that might have grown somewhat independently of that society, by and large, the two go together. As interests and their articulations in ideas followed the same course of transition and transformation the impact of interests on the seminal ideas of professional social sciences—their theoretic, ideological and professional development—is unmistakable. Without resorting to any procrustean materialist reductionist position, it may be argued that ideas and interpretations in history have been closely knit with the structures as well as dynamics of power—be they economic, political or social. Ideas were either propounded from time to time to sustain and justify a particular system of power-relations or to vocalize opposition to the existing system. Hence, the realm of ideas, concepts and theories is inseparable from the societal conditions in which they germinate, grow, flourish, and sometimes even decline.

What is true of social sciences in general is perhaps doubly true of the growth of sociology and social anthropology as academic disciplines and professions. Most of their key concepts and 'unit-ideas', such as 'sacred-secular', 'authority', 'alienation', 'anomie', 'community', 'status', 'class' etc., were products of the social transition and transformation brought about by the two 'Great Revolutions' (Nisbet, 1966: 3-44). As modern capitalism developed in western Europe from the nineteenth century onwards, sociologists began formulating ideas, concepts and theories with a view to understanding complex social realities involved in the development of capitalism as a system of social relations. With the imperialist expansion of modern capitalism, the spread of western ideas in the colonized societies was inevitable. Classical political economy—its *laissez-faire* and utilitarian principles—came to be accepted as one interpretation of the type of society founded on industrial capitalism. On the other hand, Marxist-socialist thought aimed at exposing the abominable aspects of capitalist society—its inherent contradictions reflected in class antagonism and resolved by class struggle. The latter intellectual tradition, which swept Europe in the second half of the nineteenth century, focused sharply on the links between theory, ideology and 'praxis' or between the questions: what is it? why is it? and what will it be and why should it be? (R. Mukherjee, 1977b: 2-4). Any assessment of the development of sociology and social anthropology in India cannot, therefore, be attempted without examining the overlapping of the various theoretical, methodological and ideological influences on the growth of these twin disciplines.

Growth of sociology and social anthropology in India

The colonial heritage

The expansion of western capitalism and imperialism, together with its attendant ideas and concepts, was bound for confrontation with the traditional societies which were colonized. The confrontation between the two sets of societies, their institutions and values, was most dramatic in colonies like India having a strong sense of cultural identity preserved through history. The encounter eventually became channelled into fruitful exchanges, though of unequal kind, and these ultimately led to decolonization and India's embarking on a unique road to modernization through planned development (Moore Jr., 1969: 314-410). The encounter between tradition and modernity, between the orient and the occident, in the Indian setting was mediated by a host of civil servants in the colonial administration. The rudimentary social anthropology and sociology in India were born of this initial encounter between the colonial administration to the extent that this contributed to the consolidation of the empire (Asad, 1973; Gough, 1966: 12-27, 1975).

Indian society and culture were totally unfamiliar to the colonial authorities when they first arrived. The structural aspects of caste, religious sects and their rituals and beliefs, the tribal world, the language and numerous dialects, and above all the village communities and land tenurial systems in India, all presented a baffling variety. They were too complex to be comprehended by using the relatively simple concepts and analytical categories drawn from the historical experiences of the western European societies.

The absence of a proper grasp and appreciation of Indian social realities led to severe problems in the colonial administration. Inadequate, and often inaccurate, understanding of local customs and traditions, misjudgements about different institutional arrangements were bound to disturb peace and order. For example, failure to fully appreciate the traditional social systems of land tenure resulted in a number of agrarian disturbances and revolts (Dhanagare, 1977). Placed in such a situation, the colonial administration found sociology and social anthropology to be useful instruments of colonial domination. Thus, sociology and social anthropology found much of their impetus in the contribution they could make to the smooth running of colonial administration in India. Francis Buchanan's famous travelogues written in the early nineteenth century, B.H. Baden-Powell's pioneering work on *Land System of British India*, Risley's *The Peoples of India*, studies on castes and tribes by Nesfield, W. Crook, E. Thurston and J.H. Hutton, work on the village communities by Henry Maine and Baden-Powell, Grierson's monumental *Linguistic Survey of India*, all these were inspired by the same urge for basic data and information required by the colonial administration. Most of the earlier reviews of the development of sociology and social anthropology in India have emphasized and acknowledged the impact of this colonial heritage on their growth. To cite only one of them:

> The administrative needs of the British rulers led them to collect information about the economic, social and religious life of the people. This task became increasingly complex and systematic as the nineteenth century progressed and it provided the stimulus for not only social anthropology and sociology but also Indology (Srinivas and Panini, 1973: 184).

Indigenous social thought and renaissance

This is not to suggest that there was no indigenous social thought and sociological tradition or that there were no Indian attempts to understand and interpret the complexities of the Indian tradition. Various facets of Indian society and of social change resulting from its exposure to forces of modernization stirred the minds of men. In the nineteenth century Indian renaissance, it is not very difficult to trace some elements of, what may broadly be called, indigenous sociological imagination. Religious and social reformers like Raja Rammohun Roy, Keshab Chandra Sen, Ishwar Chandra Vidyasagar, social and moral philosophers like Ramakrishna Paramhamsa and Vivekananda, political thinkers and freedom fighters like Dadabhai Naoroji, B.G. Tilak, and G.K. Gokhale, economic policy-makers like R.C. Dutt and M.G. Ranade and many others may be mentioned in this context. They all endeavoured to understand systematically different structural and cultural peculiarities of Indian society. In their own, they tried to resolve the problems Indian society faced within the framework of British rule. Ramkrishna Mukherjee (1977b: 13-15) has characterized them as "pre-sociological reference-groups of Indian sociology and social anthropology which were evolving an interpretative scheme for a proper appraisal of social reality" in India. Not that these attempts were totally free from the influence of exogenous ideas borrowed from western social sciences.

Some of these thinkers worked for a liberal-reformist and secular synthesis of Indian tradition and modernity; some of them advocated a revivalist rejection of the colonial domination of Indian society without necessarily forsaking the benevolent aspects of western education, science and technology, and above all, the liberal democratic institutions which happen to be some of the most precious gains for Indian society through its colonial experience.

The indigenous pre-sociological intellectual tradition, however, influenced the later development of Indian sociology and social anthropology only marginally. In their institutionalization and professionalization the twin disciplines were greatly influenced by the pioneering works of a number of scholar-administrators. They advanced a kind of 'mosaic theory' of Indian society and culture by focusing more on cultural diversity than on its unity. It was chiefly their concerns, styles of narration or presentation, their methods of collection and interpretation of data, and above all their conceptual frameworks that pioneers of Indian sociology emulated consciously or unconsciously (R. Mukherjee, 1977b: 22-23).

One of the key factors that served to unite the many diversities of India was the common struggle against the alien rule. Apart from the fact that the Indian National Movement developed more as a reaction to colonialism, there is no denying the fact that the Indian nationalist movement was constructive and creative in that it helped to develop a sense of national identity and self-consciousness; even intellectuals and social scientists internalized that sense of identity in no small measure. The writings of the British civilian-scholars (turned social anthropologists) or of the Indian political leaders, reformers and social thinkers also used western idiom and concepts. Such an approach created difficulties in understanding different structural and cultural features of Indian society. A relentless, and often indiscriminate, borrowing of western ideas, theories and concepts proved to be somewhat counter-productive as their grafting did not take roots in the Indian soil.

Modern sociology and social anthropology came to India as a complete package, implying a firm commitment to positivism, to methods of empirical observation and verification which were certainly not an integral part of the Indian tradition. The tension generated by the adoption of western ideas and concepts later manifested itself in a clamour for Indianizing social sciences in general, and sociology/social anthropology in particular.

The plea for indigenous sociology and social anthropology took different forms that ranged from the most liberal to the most extremist viewpoints. At the liberal end of the spectrum were those who were not hostile to using western concepts, models and analytical categories, but wanted their adaptation to suit the Indian socio-cultural setting. The liberal camp also included all those who advocated and practised Indology as the most indispensable perspective for developing an Indian sociology and social anthropology. This liberal disposition naturally received considerable encouragement. Since the plea for an Indological approach to the study of the people of India—castes and tribes, their social institutions, customs and cultural practices and so on—was not in any way detrimental to the colonial interests, it received all the necessary stimulus and official patronage. "Sometimes, native scholars and British officials engaged themselves in collaborative efforts to interpret traditions, customary religio-cultural practices and legal codes" (Kapadia, 1954: 1).

The Indological approach rested on the assumption that historically Indian society and culture are unique and that this 'contextual' specificity of Indian social realities could be grasped better through the 'texts'. The use of the Indological approach during the early formative years of Indian sociology and social anthropology is seen in the works of S.V. Ketkar, B.N. Seal, B.K. Sarkar and G.S. Ghurye (R. Mukherjee, 1977b: 30-33).

At the other end of the spectrum were the views expressed by A.K. Saran in the 1960s. A student of D.P. Mukerji, Saran later came under the influence of Anand Coomaraswamy. Saran now tends to reject the very possibility of 'social science', chiefly of sociology, because of its western moorings. He believes that acceptance of western social science would lead to permanent alienation of Indian intellectuals from their rich cultural heritage and world-view (Saran, 1958, 1962, 1962b, 1968). D.P. Mukerji himself was more tolerant of western ideas, concepts and analytical categories. When he remarked that sociologists "saturated in their own traditions" (Mukerji, 1958: 232) are at greater ease in understanding Indian society, he was really hinting at the need for an indigenous sociology and social anthropology, but he certainly did not want to insulate these disciplines in India from the western social traditions.

The history of the early development of sociology and social anthropology in India is thus punctuated by multi-level syntheses—of western theories, concepts and models and indigenous social thought and ideas. These emanated from colonial administrators, missionaries, social thinkers and social scientists.

Institutionalization: pre-1950 phase

The institutionalization and professionalization of sociology and social anthropology in India have two clearly identifiable phases—before 1950 and after. Moreover, 1950-52 is also a watershed in the sense that it was then that free India embarked on programmes of planned development.

The pre-1950 phase was essentially a phase of multi-level syntheses. It is not without significance that the twin disciplines had their beginnings in the two cities of Bombay and Calcutta which symbolically represented colonialism. These beginnings were more or less simultaneous in the second decade of the present century (R. Mukherjee, 1977b: 29-30). Initially, more established and 'grown-up' social science partners treated sociology and social anthropology as a 'residual category'. Consequently, the twin disciplines were relegated to a subordinate position in the organizational structure of Indian universities. By sheer historical accident the twin disciplines came to be included in economics departments in some universities, and in philosophy, political science, or social work in others. Even at the University of Bombay where sociology and social anthropology registered a steady progress, they formed an integral part of the Bombay School of Economics and Sociology. Later, the same pattern was adopted at the Lucknow University—another centre which was in the forefront of Indian sociology and social anthropology for a considerable period of time. When a full-fledged sociology department was started at Delhi University in the late 1950s, it was located in the Delhi School of Economics. At most of the other universities, sociology and social anthropology had a precarious existence because their teaching was confined to a course or two which post-graduate students could offer as a part of philosophy, political science, or economics curricula. The fate of sociology and social anthropology in this early period hinged partly on their perceived functional utility, and partly on how well-entrenched their "big-brothers" were in the academic power structures of their respective universities. The image of these twin disciplines had difficulty in overcoming their initial rickety constitution despite the sumptuous nourishment they received after the 1950s (Dhanagare, 1980: 24). Depending upon their association with other disciplines, sociology and social anthropology, enriched themselves by borrowing conceptual apparatus as well as tools and methodologies and also by sharing research themes or concerns of other social sciences. Above all, a stiff struggle for survival in the Indian academic milieu kept sociology and social anthropology close together so that they developed a symbiotic relationship in the early phase of their development.

In this pre-1950 phase the contributions of B.N. Seal, G.S. Ghurye, B.K. Sarkar, Radhakamal Mukherjee, D.P. Mukerji and K.P. Chattopadhyay are particularly noteworthy. Their intellectual interests, methods of data collection, and their interpretations of the Indian social system and social institutions were strongly influenced by the style and content of the ethnographic works produced by scholar-administrators during the colonial period. Studies on caste, family, marriage and kinship, social stratification, tribal communities, rural and urban society figured prominently in this period.

Sociology in Bombay developed under the leadership of G.S. Ghurye. The range of Ghurye's scholarly interests and research is astounding. Exploration of diverse aspects of Indian culture and society through the use of Indological sources permeated Ghurye's otherwise shifting intellectual concerns and empirical research pursuits. His monographs on *Indian Sadhus* (1964), on *Religious Consciousness* (1965), on *Gotra and Charan as the two Brahmanical Institutions* (1972) among others reflect that enduring concern. Ghurye also maintained the tradition established by civilian-scholars of studying castes, races and tribes in India (1943, 1963a,

1969). Later generations of Indian sociologists and social anthropologists were to use these inexhaustible themes for their researches. Although trained in the craft of Indology, Ghurye was not averse to the field-work tradition of social and cultural anthropology. His field-survey of sex-habits of middle class people in Bombay, conducted in the 1930s (Ghurye, 1938) and the monograph on the Mahadev Kolis (1963b) demonstrated that far from promoting an arm-chair textual scholarship, Ghurye introduced a down-to-earth empiricism in Indian sociology and social anthropology.

The sweep of Ghurye's works and the wide range of his intellectual interests have had a profound influence on the development of the twin disciplines in India. Like a discreet butterfly Ghurye moved from one theme to another with equal interest, erudition, and ability. He showed India to be an inexhaustible mine where sociologists and social anthropologists could conduct endless explorations. He indicated innumerable but unexplored dimensions of Indian society, culture, and social institutions which would occupy social analysts for decades if they had both the desire and the ability to 'know'. This rare spirit of inquiry and commitment to advancing the frontiers of knowledge was one of Ghurye's precious gifts to Indian sociology and social anthropology. His diversified interests are also reflected in the great variety of works his research students produced on themes ranging from family, kinship structures, marriage, religious sects, ethnic groups—castes and aboriginals, their customs and institutions, to social differentiation and stratification, caste and class, education and society, the Indian nationalist movement, social structure and social change in specific villages or regions of India, and also urbanization, industrialization and related social problems in India.

Ghurye's rigour and discipline are now legendary in Indian sociological circles. In the application of theories to empirical exercises or in the use of methodologies for data collection that legendary rigour is not somehow reflected. To put it differently: Ghurye was not dogmatic in the use of theory and methodology. He seems to have believed in practising and in encouraging disciplined eclecticism in theory and methodology. Despite his training at Cambridge under W.H.R.V. Rivers and his broad acceptance of the structural-functional approach, Ghurye did not strictly conform to the functionalist tradition when interpreting the complex facets of Indian society and culture which he chose to investigate. It would be appropriate to characterize Ghurye as a practitioner of 'theoretical pluralism'. Basically interested in inductive empirical exercises and in depicting Indian social reality using any source material—primarily Indological—his theoretical position bordered on *laissez-faire*. Similarly, when Ghurye conducted survey-type research involving primary data collection, he did not conform strictly to accepted methodological canons. He often ventured into generalizations on the basis of scanty and unrepresentative evidence (e.g., Ghurye 1968). It is also likely that Ghurye's flexible approach to theory and methodology in sociology and social anthropology was born of his faith in intellectual freedom which is reflected in the diverse theoretical and methodological approaches his research students pursued in their works.

Another important centre for social anthropological research was Calcutta University where K.P. Chattopadhyay provided the lead, and carried out a variety of research. In a way, he inherited the legacy of B.N. Seal and B.K. Sarkar who had pioneered studies on ethnicity, religion and culture (R. Mukherjee, 1977b: 31-41). However, Chattopadhyay's perspective and methods differed in more ways than one from those of his predecessors. Whereas Seal and Sarkar were products of the Bengali renaissance and were inspired by the Indian National Movement, Chattopadhyay was a Cambridge trained social anthropologist. He conducted large scale social surveys which revealed the conditions of the peasantry and the working class as well as of the tribals in Bengal and elsewhere (Chattopadhyay, 1946, 1947a, 1947b, 1952). These sections of the Indian society were being mobilized in the 1930s and 1940s not only in Bengal but also elsewhere (Dhanagare, 1975, 1976). Their newly acquired identity and consciousness, and their political awakening were reflected both in the empirical findings of Chattopadhyay (1947b) and in the kinds of policy imperatives he urged.

The growing poverty in rural Bengal, and the devastating impact of the Bengal Famine (1943) on the weaker sections—rural as well as urban—attracted his attention. Later, some of his co-workers and contemporaries pursued research on these themes with an added vigour. Ramkrishna Mukherjee's (1949, 1957, 1958) initial works on rural Bengal—its economic structure and dynamics—could be partly attributed to K.P. Chattopadhyay's initiative in portraying that side of Indian social reality of which sociologists and social anthropologists coming from urban middle class background were likely to lose sight. At the Indian Statistical Institute, Calcutta, agrarian class-structure, class relations and agrarian social change were given priority in large scale sample surveys. The theme of agrarian social structure and change was to re-appear in Indian sociology only after a gap of nearly two decades in the late 1960s and in the 1970s.

The theoretical and methodological orientation of K.P. Chattopadhyay presented a curious blend of 'diffusionist and structural-functional approach' and 'a Marxist dialectical approach'. He adopted the latter more vigorously in his later years. His initial acceptance of the former may possibly be traced to the influence of B.N. Seal and B.K. Sarkar as they too, though remotely, subscribed to structural-functional perspective. However, by the time K.P. Chattopadhyay turned to the problems of the peasantry, working class and tribals, his earlier fascination for structural-functional approach has already got attenuated giving way to a Marxist dialectical approach (R. Mukherjee, 1977b: 39-42). Interestingly enough, at Calcutta University social anthropology alone survived, although there was no formal separation between the twin disciplines and sociology had to wait for over a quarter of a century to obtain the formal status of a full-fledged university department, that came into existence only in the late 1970s. On the whole, though, Chattopadhyay's impact on Indian sociology and social anthropology remained segmental (R. Mukherjee, 1977b: 32).

Lucknow University was another major centre of sociology and social anthropology. Under the scholarship of the triumvirate—Radhakamal Mukherjee, D.P. Mukerji, and D.N. Majumdar—

Lucknow soon emerged as a leading centre for social science studies and it remained so until the mid-1960s. Radhakamal Mukherjee and D.P. Mukerji were both educated at Calcutta and had their initial training in economics. D.N. Majumdar was also a product of Calcutta but later went to Cambridge for his Ph.D with Haddon; he also attended seminars given by Malinowski at the London School of Economics. He pursued his commitment to empiricism and to the field-work tradition of social and cultural anthropology with undiminished zeal till his death in 1960. Ethnographic studies of various races and cultures in India kept Majumdar preoccupied initially although later he turned to studies of the village and of the town (Majumdar, 1955, 1958, 1960).

While there may have been some shifts in the thematic concerns of Majumdar, he remained within the structural-functionalist tradition in social anthropology. Intensive field-work and observational data formed the essential ingredients of his approach from which he did not depart even when he took to conducting large scale survey type researches. On the other hand, we find distinctive shifts in the intellectual orientations of Radhakamal Mukherjee. Having received initial training in economics, Radhakamal began with a series of micro-level analyses of problems in economic sociology, such as rural economy and land problems (1926, 1927), population problems (1938), and problems of the Indian working class (1945). In the late 1920s when the Great Depression had set in, Radhakamal initiated a number of micro-level inquiries into the deteriorating agrarian relations and conditions of the peasantry in Oudh (Mukherjee, 1929). This study should have been a pace-setter in agrarian studies in India but, except for Ramkrishna Mukherjee, who conducted a series of studies on agrarian structure in Bengal in the 1940s, this aspect of Indian rural society remained neglected till the 1960s.

After receiving training in social anthropology in England, Radhakamal Mukherjee naturally took a more active interest in micro-level empirical field investigations. These included studies on 'inter-caste tensions' and 'urbanization', particularly cities in transition (R.K. Mukherjee, 1951, 1952, 1963, 1964) and the like.

What is interesting is that his involvement in micro-empirical sociology co-existed with his predilection towards a metaphysical and multi-dimensional philosophical view of human societies and social institutions. He thought that sociology and social anthropology were bogged down by lower order empirical realities and were forgetting the higher order ones whose laws and processes governed them. He advocated and practised philosophical anthropology. In an almost meta-theoretical perspective he tended to view individual, society and values as an apparent trinity, but quintessentially an indivisible unity (R.K. Mukherjee, 1931, 1949, 1950, 1956 and 1965). In this sense, Radhakamal was the pioneer of a transdisciplinary approach in Indian social science.

D.P. Mukerji's contribution to sociology and social anthropology in India differs significantly from those of Radhakamal and D.N. Majumdar who were his contemporaries in Lucknow. Mukerji was never involved in any empirical exercises of data collection or surveys. Not that he did not believe in the inherent value of empiricism. It was just that temperamentally he preferred to be an arm-chair social critic, social philosopher, and a culturologist. His academic interests were diverse; they ranged from 'music and fine arts as peculiar creations of the Indian culture' to the 'Indian tradition in relation to modernity' (Mukerji, 1948, 1958). He was not a prolific writer like his contemporaries in Lucknow—Radhakamal and D.N. Majumdar. Yet, as an intellectual and an inspiring teacher, he left behind a powerful legacy that influenced the later generation of Indian sociologists in no small measure (R. Mukherjee, 1977b: 35).

Concerning Mukerji's approach to the understanding of Indian society, culture, and change, two points need to be stressed. First, like Radhakamal Mukerjee, he was very much against maintaining rigid barriers between one social science discipline and another; and both shared historical perspective in their studies. However, although both, like Ghurye, had an abiding interest in the study of structure and change in Indian society, in their works we do not find a new conceptual framework as such (Unnithan et al., 1965: 15-16). The similarity between the two ends there. Mukerji was a professed

Marxist, or 'Marxologist' as he preferred to call himself, and attempted a dialectical interpretation of the encounter between the Indian tradition and modernity which unleashed many forces of cultural contradiction during the colonial era (Yogendra Singh, 1973: 18-20). Within the broad spectrum of the Marxist world-view and the dialectical approach, Mukerji strove, however, to maintain the separate identity of his own views. He focused more on the historical specificity of India's cultural and social transformation which was characterized less by 'class struggle' and more by value assimilation and cultural synthesis that resulted from the encounter between tradition and modernity (see Madan, 1977: 167-8).

It was D.P. Mukerji who first cogently stressed the need for sociologists to turn their attention from description and analysis to prescriptive solutions that emanate only from deep convictions and value-choices as well as from ideological predilections about a preferred future. In that sense he explored the myth of 'value-freeness' of the social sciences. However, it should be pointed out that except for few (like P.C. Joshi and S.C. Verma), none of his students (A.K. Saran, Yogendra Singh, S.P. Nagendra, Indra Deva, among others) subscribed to his Marxian framework of analysis. This clearly shows that, far from being either dogmatic or doctrinnaire, he put a high value on intellectual freedom.

That intellectual freedom is a precondition for an advancement of science and of the frontiers of knowledge was the basic faith of the founding fathers of Indian sociology and social anthropology. This explains why, despite their own preferences for certain perspectives and methodologies, their students could contribute appreciably to the development of alternative conceptual framework for studying Indian society—its structure and change in the post-1950 period.

Expansion of teaching and research: post-1950 period

In the pre-1950 phase there were only a few centres of study in sociology and social anthropology besides Bombay, Calcutta and Lucknow. At the Deccan College, Post-graduate and Research Institute, Pune, the department of sociology and social anthropology was started in 1939 under Irawati Karve. Despite her own sustained work, her department hardly expanded till 1952-53 when an additional post of lecturer in sociology was created. The situation in most of the colleges and universities which introduced teaching of sociology/social anthropology was no different.

Being Ghurye's student, Irawati Karve inherited some of his research concerns and methodology. Her interests centered around kinship structures (Karve, 1953), ethnic groups and castes and peculiarities of the regional culture in western India. She carried out numerous studies in physical anthropology, using anthropometric techniques of measurement. Like Ghurye, she too used Indological sources extensively to reinterpret the Hindu society (Karve, 1968), social institutions, symbolism of ritual and values as well as folk-songs, legends and epics (Malhotra, 1971: 26-36) and was equally committed to the typical cultural anthropological tradition of field-work and observational data. Above all, she was no less eclectic in theory and methodology than her teacher Ghurye. As we shall later see, research problems, interests and methods underwent significant change at the Deccan College, Pune in the 1960s and 1970s when another distinguished student of Ghurye, Y.B. Damle, attempted to base sociological inquiries in rigorous theory and methodology and explored new dimensions of structure and change in Indian society (Damle, 1971: 41-43).

The real phase of expansion of sociology and social anthropology began in 1952. Several factors account for a phenomenal expansion and growth of the twin disciplines during the past three decades or so. First, the policy-makers of independent India pursued objectives of economic regeneration and social development, and they recognized the role of the social sciences in attaining the objectives of national reconstruction and development. Since the policy-makers rightly viewed education and development as interrelated, different branches of the social sciences assumed importance and received impetus after 1950. Their efforts were aimed primarily at revealing "variations of different societal phenomena as well as the interrelationships among them" (R. Mukherjee,

1977b: 45). The Government of India had officially undertaken programmes of planned development—its first Five Year Plan started in 1952—and sociology and social anthropology were seen as sources of possible expertise on 'social aspects of development—its determinants and consequences'. These would not normally fall within the purview of economists who not only gained considerable status and approbation in the government's policy-making bodies but also dominated universities where other social science departments were accumulating data that could also be used by social planners. The main consumers of social science data were the government and its numerous agencies. The Research Programmes Committee of the Planning Commission provided most of the finances required for research projects of social scientists. The need to study the impact of development programmes on different sections of society, and for programme evaluation was so great that it created a considerable increase in the demand for trained personnel in sociology and social anthropology (Srinivas and Panini, 1973: 197-8; Atal, 1976: 149-50).

The growth in general awareness of the relevance of the twin disciplines for development and planning activities was reflected in the development grants for starting new departments or expanding existing university departments given by the University Grants Commission (UGC). This euphoria of 'development' explains to a large extent the institutionalization and expansion of sociology and social anthropology in Indian universities after 1950. To facilitate this expansion so that universities and their departments could perform the task of providing information, the UGC sanctioned new posts in several universities through Five Year Plan development grants.

In this phase of expansion, Indian sociology and social anthropology looked primarily to western social sciences for their theoretic and methodological orientations. Conceptual and analytical models were freely borrowed and applied. The indiscriminate borrowing was not a new experience for the twin disciplines in India. In the post-1950 phase attempts were made to adapt the borrowed frameworks and research tools or to find substitute for them. In the pre-1950 period, Indian sociology and social anthropology had followed the dominant trends in British social and cultural anthropology, particularly B. Malinowski's functionalism with its culturological strain. After 1950, however, in addition to British social anthropology, Indian sociology and social anthropology found a still closer ally in American rural sociology (R. Mukherjee, 1977b: 47). What facilitated the development of these contacts was the acceptance of the ideology and a programme of community development by the Indian government.

Between 1951 and 1970, the Ford Foundation in India succeeded in transplanting the idea of community development into Indian planning. Its indispensability as a crucial instrument of social reconstruction and as an agency of development, particularly in rural areas, was accepted by the Indian government. It was this package of community development that opened up job opportunities for Indian social scientists in general and sociologists and social anthropologists in particular. They could secure funds for research projects to study Indian villages, to investigate the impact of the community development programmes and the response of villages to the development programmes. Large-scale surveys had to be undertaken to provide data that would meet the requirements of the administrator. This required Indian sociologists and social anthropologists to get acquainted with modern survey research methods and procedures of empirical social science developed in the West, particularly in the United States. To meet these demands, courses on research methodology were introduced into the teaching of sociology and social anthropology in India (Beteille, 1973: 224-31). So pressing were the demands on social science research to produce data relevant for planning and development administration that Indian sociologists and social anthropologists hardly had the time or the inclination to reflect on substantive issues in 'methodology'; what came to pass, to be taught and practised under the label of 'methodology' was plain and simple 'research technology'.

The community development programme did in many ways facilitate the growth and expansion of the twin disciplines in India but in quantitative rather than qualitative terms. Since under the government patronage the twin disciplines were mostly at the receiving end, they could not come of age in the true sense of the term. Like an aged infant they failed to develop their own identity even after the 1950s. Unfortunately, several side-effects of the twin disciplines' preoccupation bordering on obsession with the community development were ignored. In a way this preoccupation stereotyped research themes and priorities in Indian sociology and social anthropology for nearly two decades. It was primarily the official patronage and the Ford Foundation largesse which attracted a number of sociologists and social anthropologists to this area of study. There was nothing inherently wrong with this growing-edge of twin disciplines. The problem was that research priorities were practically dictated by the state whose action as well as policy concerns came to be echoed in social science seminars and conferences (Dhanagare, 1980: 25-26).

There is another significant side-effect of community development on Indian sociology and social anthropology. The degree of proximity to the state and government's policy formulating bodies became an index of academic status and recognition. The new status criteria transformed the earlier interaction between two or more disciplines into an almost pathological competition for resources as well as recognition.

Economics, with its rigour and precision in measurement, naturally enjoyed pride of place in the family of social sciences (Srinivas and Panini, 1973: 199) while sociology and social anthropology, with their omnibus character, were relegated to a subsidiary status which the practitioners of these disciplines tended to accept (R. Mukherjee, 1977b: 45). Occasionally, they did react to the situation when they staked their claims to serve as policy planners, advisers and experts (Saksena, 1964; and Damle, 1974: 344).

The competition among various social sciences to woo the establishment did not allow any useful dialogue to take place among them. The consequences of this are not far to seek: social sciences became compartmentalized and disciplinary boundaries were drawn as rigidly as possible. Paradoxically, while there was considerable talk of an 'interdisciplinary approach' and a need for interdisciplinary studies, until 1970 or so, narrow disciplinary interests prevented any promotion of interdisciplinary work. Not only were sociology and social anthropology estranged from economics, history, political science and philosophy with which they had either co-existed and indeed interacted in the pre-1950 period, but also, in this process, sociology and social anthropology which maintained a very productive and symbiotic relationship during the pre-1950 phase became estranged from each other. And yet in the 1960s and 1970s the trend was clearly in favour of a separation of sociology and social anthropology in most of the Indian universities except for Bombay and Saugar. The newly started central universities, like JNU (New Delhi), NEHU (Shillong), and Hyderabad favoured the older pattern by setting up a joint department of sociology and social anthropology although NEHU has already succumbed to the pressure for separation. Even where the two lived together, their wedlock was not free from tension. The trend of the interrelationship between sociology and social anthropology in post-1950 period could be summed up thus. Where the two became more or less completely merged without pedantic debate on lines of demarcation etc., the fusion undoubtedly produced the best results in terms of the enrichment of both. This could not be better exemplified than by the advances made by sociology departments at Bombay, Poona, Saugar, and Delhi universities. In Delhi, although sociology and anthropology were separate departments from the beginning, the department of sociology emphasized social anthropology. Where the two went their separate ways they did not do so on genuine academic grounds and consequently both suffered, although the losses to 'anthropology' tended to be heavier. Without interaction with sociology, anthropology was invariably reduced to ethnology and physical anthropologists and social/cultural anthropologists had little in common except shared office-space and administrative and financial control.

For these reasons, the relationship between sociology and

social anthropology in India today remains characterized by ambivalence. Sociologists who have research interests similar to those of anthropologists frequently prefer a self-imposed isolation or conveniently demarcated boundaries. On the other hand, career social anthropologists in sociology profession do not normally like to be identified as 'anthropologists'. Interestingly enough, although the Indian Council of Social Science Research (ICSSR), set up by Government of India in 1969, decided to conduct a combined survey (trend reports) on sociology and social anthropology in India, the Council maintained, for some years, separate panels of experts for sociology and social anthropology. At the UGC the situation is no different.

Establishment of the ICSSR in 1969 contributed considerably to the growth of sociology and social anthropology in India. It more or less took over the functions of the Research Programmes Committee of the Planning Commission. As an autonomous body, the Council is financially independent and it has supported several university departments through funds for research projects, seminars and workshops, publication of books and journals, data-analysis and consultancy, and also for short or long-term fellowships both for junior and senior members of the profession. ICSSR's many schemes were sufficiently broad-based as well as egalitarian to inspire confidence among all social scientists including sociologists and social anthropologists. It has played a positive and constructive role in the development of sociology and social anthropology in India since the late 1960s.

Research trends (1950-79)

In the pre-1950 phase of Indian sociology and social anthropology, a broad concern for understanding Indian social and cultural realities permeated the profession. Studies of caste, family, kinship, races and cultures, and religious beliefs, values and practices were vigorously pursued. Research on these themes was influenced by the works of colonial administrator-scholars. Theoretically, Malinowski's functionalism and culturological perspective found a wide acceptance, although very few cared to adopt it more rigorously. The dialectical perspective on Indian society and culture was not treated as sacrosanct. Some scholars approached Indian social institutions from a historical and Indological standpoint. Survey research was less common; macro-analytical exercises were preferred to micro-sociological and social anthropological research.

Although a good deal of change has taken place in Indian sociology and social anthropology since the 1950s, not all the research concerns of the earlier days have been abandoned. In fact, the continuity of research concerns is striking. New trends emerged too, but the older ones came to be consolidated in the 1950s and the 1960s. Chief among them are themes such as caste and stratification, family and kinship, religion and ritual, and village social organization. These continued to preoccupy sociologists and social anthropologists. Above all, caste and stratification proved to be such an overridingly important structural reality in Indian society that it continued to captivate the bulk of Indian sociologists and social anthropologists (Srinivas, et al., 1959a). But, even in this persistent trend of caste and stratification studies, a qualitative difference is to be noticed in research on this theme conducted in recent years.

Srinivas's studies of caste and religion (1952, 1959, 1962, 1966) highlighted not only their structural-functional aspects, but also the dynamics of the caste system in rural setting. He proposed conceptual tools like 'dominant caste', 'Sanskritization-Westernization' and 'secularization' to understand the realities of inter-caste relations and to explain their dynamics (Srinivas, 1956, 1959, 1962, 1966, 1968). The concept of dominant caste has been used widely in the study of power relations at the village level. Y.B. Damle (1968: 95-102) advocated the use of reference-group theory in explaining caste mobility and dynamics, whereas Andre Beteille, in his study of a Tanjore village, found the Weberian framework of 'caste, class and power' (1965) useful in analyzing the complexities of the changing social stratification system in Indian villages. To him, movements of castes may be seen along three axes: 'Ritual status' (which is structurally defined); 'class position' (which is decided by relation to means of production or by the nature of control over economic resources); and 'political power'. Although interrelated, these three foci are irreducible in the study and understanding of the complex and changing reality of Indian stratification system.

Louis Dumont's *Homo Hierarchicus* (1970) to some extent revived the interest in 'caste' studies in the 1970s. He focused on the need to understand the ideology of caste as reflected in the classical texts. Dumont advocated the use of an Indological and structuralist approach to the study of caste system and village social structure in India.

Different facets of caste and stratification system attracted the attention of sociologists and social anthropologists. Political developments in India through the dispensations of the community development, panchayati raj, and democratic decentralization after the early 1950s had far-reaching social consequences. Their impact on rural social structure, power structure and rural change attracted considerable attention for nearly two decades (S.C. Dube, 1969; R.N. Haldipur, 1974: 30-165). Hence, studies on caste and power structure in rural society figured more prominently. Studies by Yogendra Singh (1969b), A. Beteille (1969), B.S. Baviskar (1968, 1969), C. Parvathamma (1964, 1968) and many others could be cited in this context. As Baviskar (1974: 431-507) has observed in this area of the sociology of politics, major contributions have come from professional political scientists (for example, Kothari, 1970a, 1970b; Sirsikar 1970).

The role of caste in politics, particularly at the village or local level, was a very common theme in the early stages of political sociology in India. This is reflected in the works of Srinivas, Andre Beteille, Yogesh Atal and many others. Interest in this line of research was sustained mostly by foreign scholars like A.C. Mayer, Kathleen Gough, F.G. Bailey, Harold Gould, Mckim Marriott and several others. Dumont and Pocock's *Contributions to Indian Sociology* (old series) provided a forum which gave further impetus to that interest. Later, studies on the role of dominant caste in village politics by Dube (1968), Atal (1968), Oommen (1970) and others revived that interest.

Another theme in political sociology was studies on political parties and political associations. But here too, except for M.S.A. Rao's (1968, 1979a) and Anil Bhat's (1970) works, most of the studies were undertaken by professional political scientists, not few of whom are foreigners. Other conventional interests in political sociology revolved around 'factionalism' and its role in the developmental process. Studies by Baviskar (1980) and Rastogi (1964, 1967) may be mentioned in this context, although it would be fair to say that contributions to this area again came more prominently from Indian political scientists and sociologists and social anthropologists from abroad.

The emergence of 'elites' at different levels of the power-structures received some attention in the works of S.K. Lal (1974) and more recently Sachchidanada (1977).

A somewhat new and unconventional line of research in political sociology is evident in an innovative study by Yogesh Atal (1971b). Although a number of sociologists tried their hand in election studies, this was the first systematic empirical investigation in which Atal used a 'panel-study' design, interviewed voters in three waves to reveal the communication links between the local communities and national level politics and the degrees of citizen's political awareness and participation (Atal, 1969, 1971b). Equally new is the study of political socialization of school children undertaken by Surendra Gupta (1975).

Closely related to studies on caste and stratification and power politics have been 'village studies' or 'rural studies' which constituted another important area of interest. In the colonial era, villages—their caste structures, social arrangement on land and so on—attracted considerable attention from scholars, and administrators alike. The post-1950 period marks a watershed in the studies of rural communities in India (Chauhan, 1974: 83). S.C. Dube's *Indian Village* (1955) was a significant work in this period in the sense that it was the first full-length account of a village social structure. Dube depicted rural social structure and institutions in his characteristically lucid style, and the work served as a model for descriptive-exploratory accounts of several other micro-settings that came to be studied later. But Dube did not offer any analytical insights, nor did he propose any alternative conceptual framework for studying Indian rural society

Interest in rural studies grew steadily largely because of the acceptance of the community development programme by the Government of India. This necessitated a shift from 'structure' to 'change' in India's villages. Dube's other pioneering work *India's Changing Villages* (1958) as well as two volumes edited by M. Marriott (1955) and M.N. Srinivas (1960) present the results of a number of such studies on the structure and change in the village society. Subsequently, a large number of scholars undertook village studies. Earlier, in the 1940s, Ramkrishna Mukherjee had studied the economic structure of six villages in Bengal (1949, 1958). This tradition of studying a group of villages was continued by Yogendra Singh (1969a b), K.L. Sharma (1970, 1974) and others, for it provided a better data base needed for a more representative study and for more tenable generalizations. However, studies of a single village or comparisons of two villages from different settings continued. B.R. Chauhan's (1967)*A Rajasthan Village* and Yogesh Atal's (1968) comparative study of caste in two villages from Madhya Pradesh and Rajasthan respectively, could be cited as examples among several others.

To this area of village studies, sociologists and social anthropologists contributed alike although they focused on different dimensions. For example, K.S. Mathur (1964) investigated the ritual aspects of caste in a Malwa village, whereas T.N. Madan (1965) drew attention to the structure and function of domestic groups within the wider kinship network of a selected caste group in a village setting. Although Madan's work does not belong to the category of 'village studies' in the strict sense, it was carried out in a Kashmir village nonetheless. G. Chattopadhyaya's (1964) account of Ranjana village in West Bengal or M.S.A. Rao's study of political and economic changes in a village on the fringe of metropolitan Delhi (Rao, 1970) are yet other examples. So popular was this area of research that researchers came to be identified with the villages they studied. Srinivas's Rampura, Dube's Shamirpet, Andre Beteille's Sripuram, or K. Ishwaran's (1967) Shivapur became almost legendary pairs of names. Since the 1950s, several foreign scholars—mostly British and American social anthropologists—have also devoted themselves to studying the structural and institutional complexities of Indian rural society. All these contributions have left behind a powerful, and equally popular, legacy of field-work for collecting observational depth data. Although the focus may change, Indian villages will continue to occupy a central place in the research concerns of sociologists and social anthropologists in the future.

Studies of social mobility among different castes were also carried out and these demonstrated a convergence of interests in rural studies, stratification studies and studies of social change. Here the focus was mainly on social forces which accounted for social mobility among different castes. In this area, contributions of A. Beteille (1969), R.S. Khare (1970), Sunanda Patwardhan (1968), and K.C. Alexander (1968) are particularly noteworthy. This research interest took sociologists and social anthropologists 'beyond the village' and led them to investigate patterns of changes in urban settings as Satish Saberwal (1976) did. Social mobility among the Scheduled Castes, Scheduled Tribes and Backward Classes in India also received considerable attention during the 1960s (Sachchidananda, 1974: 276-310). The Indian Council of Social Science Research has shown particular interest in sponsoring a series of surveys of the weaker sections of society with a view to reveal the impact of various development measures and welfare programmes of the state on their educational, social, and occupational status. Results of some of these are being published and it will be sometime before it is possible to undertake a comparative study bringing out the patterns of social mobility and change among these sections in the whole of India.

In the post-1950 period, professional social anthropologists have been concerned with the study of tribal societies—tribal villages, their economy, marriage, family and kinship structures, their customs, traditions and folklore—as well as change in tribal societies resulting from the impact of Christianity or other reform movements, modern political developments or social welfare measures of the state (Vidyarthi, 1972: 31-104). These research interests of social anthropologists were substantively similar to those of sociologists who often shared the former's methodology and concepts. However, many social anthropologists in India have been preoccupied with studies of the material culture of tribals, or tribal folklore and art or music (ICSSR, 1972 III). These research concerns have not been shared by professional sociologists except for Srinivas who wrote articles in the 1940s on Tamil and Telugu folk-songs, and more recently Indra Deva who has done some sustained work in folklore studies (Deva, 1953; 1972: 197-239).

Sociology of kinship, marriage and family is an important area of specialization. Professional sociologists and social anthropologists in India have contributed a great deal through their research not only during the early stages of the pre-1950 period, but also during the development phase thereafter. Initially, the institutional and value-structures associated with marriage and family in different parts of India were studied. Works by Srinivas (1942, 1952), K.M. Kapadia (1955, 1956) and others may be mentioned in this context. The role of kinship, structure of kinship, its network, kinship terminology and organization were also studied by U.R. Ehrenfels (1941), Irawati Karve (1953), T.N. Madan (1965), and Leela Dube (1969) among others. The matrilineal kinship system in Malabar was studied by Kathleen Gough (1961); Leela Dube (1974) examined its interaction with Islam in the South Indian setting. The studies broke new ground in the study of marriage and family in India.

Change in family structure—its transformation from 'joint to nuclear'—as a result of urbanization and industrialization, were also studied by Kapadia (1955, 1956, 1959), I.P. Desai (1956, 1964), and M.S. Gore (1968). They all focused on the dynamics of family change and used modern survey methods to assess the nature and extent of change undergone by the institution and values of marriage and family in India. Gore used the systems analytical framework in his study. Within a broad structural-functionalist frame, A.M. Shah (1962, 1964, 1968) attempted to depict the changing dimensions of family. A rigorous study to measure kinship-distance and extent of change in family structures in West Bengal using systematic quantitative methodology was carried out by Ramakrishna Mukherjee (1972, 1977).

It may be stated here that in general, research interest in marriage, family and kinship structures is declining particularly among younger sociologists and social anthropologists. This may be partly because of their dissatisfaction with this trend in Indian sociology which they find inadequate for a proper appraisal of social reality (R. Mukherjee, 1977: 95). To some extent, the younger generation in Indian sociology, as remarked by Leela Dube (1974: 327), seems to be unwilling to go through the painstaking process of conceptual and methodological learning required in the area of family and kinship studies.

Some significant work in the field of industrial sociology has been done since the 1950s. The interest of Indian sociologists and social anthropologists in this field does not, however, show the same intensity as it does in other areas. With the growth of industrialization in India one might have expected problems related to that process to figure more prominently in sociological researches. This is not to suggest that the works available in this area are not worthy of mention. N.R. Sheth's work (1968) is particularly important. He analyzed the structure of relationships among people working in a factory in relation to the social and cultural milieu in which they live and work. A student of M.N. Srinivas, Sheth closely followed the conceptual categories associated with the structural-functional analysis. To a certain extent this is also true of B.S. Baviskar's work on the role of caste in the political/power structure within the organizational framework of a co-operative sugar factory (Baviskar, 1968: 300-15; 1969: 148-67; 1980).

Among other topics studied in the field of industrial sociology in India are: the social effects of industrialization, workers commitment, worker-management relations, job satisfaction, formal and informal groups in relation to work productivity and trade unionism. Initially, as in other areas of specializations, the lead came from foreign scholars even in this field. A mention must be made here of Richard Lambert's study (1963) on industrial workers in Poona. Professional psychologists, industrial economists, management and social work experts have also contributed to this field. However, studies on trade unions by S.D. Punekar (1948, 1967), S.M. Pandey (1967, 1968) and E.A. Ramaswami (1969, 1977) are some of the important contributions from professional sociologists.

More recently, studies on industrial entrepreneurship have been conducted by some sociologists (for example, K.L. Sharma, 1975, 1978; Saberwal, 1977). This branch of industrial sociology is likely to attract more attention from Indian sociologists in the years to come. The signs of such a trend are already visible in several client-oriented studies carried out by the Indian Institutes of Management at Ahmedabad, Bangalore and Calcutta. Some of these studies are published (see bibliography in Sheth, 1974). These institutes have sociological research units that have focused on industrial sociology, and more particularly on entrepreneurship, worker-management relations, worker commitment and productivity and so on. Needless to say a typical management orientation dominates their studies.

Three points need to be emphasized about the development of industrial sociology in India. First, this field has a tremendous potential for interdisciplinary work although at present it is contributed to more significantly by psychologists, social workers and management scientists than by sociologists and social anthropologists. This fact is also revealed by another review of studies in this area (Sheth, 1974: 158-232). Secondly, in studying problems of industrial relations, work organizations and so on, analysts have so far drawn heavily on western models, theories and conceptual categories. And lastly, there has so far been little development of either alternative conceptual frameworks or of theory-building by Indian sociologists and social anthropologists.

Urban sociology constitutes another important field in which Indian sociologists and social anthropologists have shown sustained interest and involvement. In the pre-1950 phase, pioneers like Ghurye, Radhakamal Mukherjee, K.P. Chattopadhyay and others were interested in city-studies or surveys. D.N. Majumdar, among social anthropologists of the post-1950 phase, also studied the growth of Kanpur City. After 1950, there was a considerable development in urban studies. This was largely because the Research Programmes Committee of the Planning Commission identified urban studies as a priority area and funded studies on the growth and development of specific cities as well as of the process of urbanization in different regions. The latter have been carried out mostly on the basis of census data (Balsara 1964; Sovani 1966; Bose 1970; Mitra 1967). Whether in city-studies or in studies of the urbanization process, however, economists and urban geographers dominated the scene in the post-1950 phase (D'Souza, 1974: 118-21).

It is largely in studying the nature of urban-rural contact, influence of the city on its hinterland, and socio-cultural concomitants of urbanizations that sociologists and social anthropologists have taken the lead. The analytical framework was mostly drawn from the Chicago School tradition in general and from the pioneering works of Robert E. Park, Burgess, Robert Redfield, Louis Worth, and Oscar Lewis in particular. One of the early efforts in this area is by Y.B. Damle (1955) who showed that the modernizing influence of cities on their hinterland villages is rather small in Indian setting. The impact of urbanization and industrialization on tribals has also received some attention. Gouranga Chattopadhyaya (1969) conducted a study to test whether values and behavioural norms of tribal groups are more in conformity with those of non-tribal groups. Towns in tribal setting in the Banswara region of the southern part of Rajasthan studied by Brij Raj Chauhan (1972), studies of tribal villages in Bihar by Sachchidananda (1964, 1968) and L.P. Vidyarthi (1967, 1970) are works on tribes in relation to the process of urbanization.

An important trend in urban sociology in India is represented by a large number of studies on specific towns and cities. Noteworthy among these is the study of Chandigarh by Victor D'Souza (1968) which focuses on the impact of planning, designing and architecture, in short, of physical environment on urban social structure. Bopegamage's work (1955) on Delhi, N.K. Bose's study (1968) of Calcutta, and C. Rajagopalan's works (1960, 1962) on Greater Bombay are other notable contributions. Studies of slums conducted by A.R. Desai and Devadas Pillai (1972), and by Victor D'Souza (1970: 70-74) constitute a separate category within the area of city studies. One would normally expect studies on slums to develop concomitantly with urban studies but good studies on the social background of slum-dwellers, patterns of their settlement, slum organization and so on are very few.

Sociology of education also developed in India for the most part after 1950. Expansion of educational facilities and institutions at all levels and growing awareness of the role education plays in development and social change were largely responsible for attracting the attention of sociologists and social anthropologists. In a review of some eighty-nine empirical studies done in this field, Suma Chitnis (1974: 166-216) found that researchers raised questions pertaining particularly to the role of education in socialization, expansion and growth of education, educational and stratificatory systems, education as a system and subsystem—its goals, procedures, and practices, problems of education among the weaker sections of society—and so on. Some researchers focused on the role of teachers and youth, the social background of entrants in selected institutions and the impact of power-politics on educational development. Notable contributions in this area have been made by I.P. Desai (1953, 1967), Y.B. Damle (1967, 1970), M.S. Gore (1965, 1967), S. Chitnis (1969), and B.V. Shah (1960, 1965, 1968). These sociologists have shown a sustained interest in the field of sociology of education. There are many others who have written articles on some aspects of educational sociology although such writings in this field seldom rise above the level of enlightened journalism. Those who have used systematic survey methods in research have been strongly influenced by the systems approach or perspective which is reflected in the volume edited by Gore and others (1967). Educational problems of the weaker sections of society including those of the Scheduled Castes and Scheduled

Tribes have been studied recently by a series of research projects sponsored by ICSSR. The survey carried out in several states of India has resulted into a number of monographs, some of which have been published as independent books such as Chitnis (1977), Lal (1978), Singhi (1979), and Pimpley (1980).

A new trend in sociological research developed in the 1960s and 1970s in the area of rural sociology. The new interests centered on basic changes in the rural social structure initiated through land reform measures since independence. Whereas earlier studies on Indian rural society focused mainly on the structural aspects, the new trend highlighted class formation among the peasantry, social mobility among different rural strata and the newly developing contradictions in the countryside. In some ways this is a renewal of interests in the study of the economic structure of rural society. Moreover, this new trend turned from 'micro' level inquiries to 'macro' level analytical exercises (Yogendra Singh, 1977: 22-23). To some extent, this renewed interest in agrarian studies must be attributed to A.R. Desai's (1969: 1-99) *Rural Sociology in India*—an anthology that was a major turning point and pace-setter. Another major contribution to this field of 'agrarian sociology' came from P.C. Joshi (1969, 1975) who examined historically the impact of land reforms on rural society in India. Similarly, studies of caste and class composition of agrarian social structure and of contradictions arising from processes of change were also carried out (Beteille, 1974; R. Singh, 1974; Chakravarti, 1975). These included works on rural transition and transformation—mainly in agrarian relations—resulting from community development (A.R. Desai, 1961, 1969: 611-21) or from the Green Revolution in some areas (Oommen 1975, 1977; Mencher, 1978; Alexander, 1975).

Closely related to the new trend in agrarian sociology has been the trend of studying social movements, particularly among the peasantry. Sociology of social movements remained for long a neglected area. A.R. Desai's (1948) study of the Indian National Movement—its class character and inherent contradictions—was of course a noteworthy and pioneering contribution from the pre-1950 era. T.K. Oommen (1972) studied the socio-economic reform movement of Sarvodaya and the impact of the charismatic movement on rural social structures, values and changes. In the 1970s, however, studies focused more on movements of the peasantry, historical processes of their development, the structural settings in which various peasant movements and mobilization developed, their ideologies, leadership and class character (D.N. Dhanagare, 1974, 1975a, 1975b, 1976, 1977; P.N. Mukherjee, 1977, 1978; R. Singh, 1978). Studies on peasant struggles have also been carried out by historians and social scientists of diverse orientations. Some of their works have been included in an anthology recently edited by A.R. Desai (1979). In general, the interest in the study of social movements is growing and this is evident in the two volumes recently edited by M.S.A. Rao (1978-1979) and also in his own recent work (1979a).

One of the relatively less developed areas of sociology and social anthropology is the sociology of development and economic development more particularly. Studies, though few, have covered such aspects as the role of elites in economic development (Joshi, 1968; Atal, 1968), the role of community development projects in the development process as a whole (Dube, 1964, 1966; Gaikwad, 1969; Singhi, 1974). The extent to which religion, value-systems and other cultural variables influence economic development has also been studied (Dube, 1966; Ratna Dutta, 1968; 1971; Rao, 1969; Saran, 1962).

The sociology of economic development is an area where a good deal of policy research needs to be done. Similarly, the impact of capitalist agriculture on rural development needs to be investigated by sociologists. Past work in this area reveals serious deficiencies (Dube, 1974: 19-20) which need to be overcome by systematic and imaginative research.

The field of sociology of law is not yet fully developed. Although there are individual contributions by a small number of scholars, "the subject is yet to find its feet in India" (Das, 1974: 367-400). The same holds true for sociology of medicine (Ahluwalia 1974: 421-22). To the area of sociology of religion, there are some notable contributions from social anthropologists (Sinha,

1974: 508-580) but we are yet to see a better work than Srinivas's *Religion and Society among the Coorgs of South India* (1952) from an Indian sociologist. There is a tremendous potential for investigating religious values and rituals—their meaning in contemporary society and impact of secularization. It is rather intriguing that this field continues to be neglected today. Since the International Women's Year (1975) there is a renewed interest in the field of 'women studies' and quite a few sociologists have been working on problems of women, their status and roles and so on.

Sociology of deviance—studies on crime, juvenile delinquency and so on (often called 'criminology')—grew under the umbrella of sociology for sometime. As long as sociology and social work developed under the same organizational structure, criminology was a very popular branch of sociology, but social work orientation estranged criminology from sociological perspectives and concerns. Similarly with demography, which came to be dominated by statisticians and trained demographers, population studies in India never developed as an integral part of the mainstream of sociology or social anthropology.

'Social change' as a theme continues to be a significant concern of Indian sociologists and social anthropologists. This holds true not only for the pre-1950 phase but also for post-1950 period. Srinivas (1966) attempted to construct a macro-level analysis using a large number of micro-level findings on the processes of 'Sanskritization', 'Westernization', and 'Secularization'. Yogendra Singh (1973) carried out a somewhat deductive exercise using a systematic framework. Interestingly enough, Srinivas returned to his micro-empirical setting—a village after nearly a quarter of century and in a diachronic frame highlighted the nature of social change in that village over a period of time (Srinivas, 1977).

As regards the theoretical orientations of Indian sociologists and social anthropologists, it may be said that the appeal of 'philosophical theoretical orientation' (*a la* Radhakamal Mukerjee), and 'structural-functional' and 'culturological' approach (*a la* Radcliffe Brown, M.N. Srinivas etc.) is declining. Dialectical historical orientation—often based on Marxist methods and propositions—has, of late, shown a profound capacity for adaptation and innovation (Singh, 1977: 25-26). This orientation now finds wider acceptance among the younger generation of sociologists. Marxist anthropology *per se* is yet to develop. Competing with the Marxist orientation is the 'structuralist' approach which is no less adaptive and innovative. In the works of J.P.S. Uberoi (1974, 1978), T.N. Madan (1975), and Veena Das (1977) structural analysis is evident and this trend is likely to gain further momentum in the 1980s (M.S.A. Rao, 1979b: 1812). The systemic theoretic orientation is seen in some of the writings of M.S. Gore, Yogendra Singh, Y.B. Damle, Yogesh Atal and a few others but no significant advances have been made on this front in more recent years. P.N. Rastogi continues to be the lone follower of the cybernetic approach (Rastogi, 1973, 1975).

To Ramkrishna Mukherjee, the theoretical orientations of Indian sociologists have so far carried strong value-loads and ideological preferences. Since their ideological differences are irreconcilable, there is resistance to co-ordination of theories and research. Thus, meta-academic considerations and pressures towards conformity prevent any theory construction and objective assessment of social reality. He is optimistic that such an assessment is possible by adopting, what he calls, an inductive inferential approach, i.e., by building 'inductive sociology' in which mathematical thinking and the statistical logic of inductive probability could be brought to bear on the discipline of sociology (R. Mukherjee, 1977: 130-35). What is surprising is the fact that not many share Ramkrishna Mukherjee's optimism and his rigorous approach to the understanding of social reality in India.

Demographic profile of the profession

As discussed earlier, before 1950 few Indian universities had teaching departments in sociology and social anthropology. Moreover, teaching was mainly at post-graduate level and these disciplines were almost non-existent at under-graduate level except in the form of subsidiary courses for students offering economics, politics, philosophy and so on. This meant that very few professional sociologists found academic posts because opportunities for gainful employment were scarce. At the same time, there were not many university departments to provide trained sociologists and social anthropologists. In the 1940s and early 1950s, the job situation for trained social scientists was quite precarious. Although the few sociology and social anthropology departments could hardly be held guilty of intellectual over-production, the development potential and resources of universities and other educational institutions were so restricted that some outstanding products of reputed centres like Bombay, Calcutta and Lucknow had to be content with a meagre research-fellowship here or there. Those of them who obtained even a temporary position of a lecturer in a university were considered as the lucky ones.

Several factors contributed to the expansion of the profession of sociology and social anthropology in India. First, the Government of India itself recognized the role of social sciences in the nation-building and the development process. Social scientists came to be called upon to participate in policy formation and programme evaluation. The recognition came to them mainly because social scientists provided useful data through their research and also supplied trained social science personnel to staff a wide variety of development and welfare agencies. In this regard, sociologists and social anthropologists coming out of Indian universities were at some advantage vis-a-vis their colleagues from sister disciplines, since the former were equipped with the craft of survey research, field-work, data collection, i.e., research technology in general. Secondly, to facilitate the creation of new departments, or additional posts in the existing ones, the UGC made funds available. The Planning Commission, and later the ICSSR, offered generous grants to various social science departments for research projects. Thirdly, quite a few young sociologists and social anthropologists had the opportunity to go abroad, particularly to the United States in the 1950s and 1960s for further studies, where assistantships were then available. Moreover, sociology was introduced as an optional subject at the under-graduate level in several universities from the mid 1950s onwards. This naturally opened up new avenues for employment for many young aspiring sociologists and social anthropologists in India.

A growing awareness that research is an important component of development strategies led to the creation of a number of research centres and institutions either through state financing or public initiative. Tribal research institutes, institutes of regional or development studies and the like further improved the employment prospects of sociologists and social anthropologists. The Indian Sociological Society has about 750 life members today and of these nearly 600 are Indians; the rest are foreigners. This should suffice to illustrate the growth of the profession in demographic terms.

Teaching at university and post-graduate level

A recent review (UGC, 1979) of sociology and social anthropology in India shows that out of about 120 universities and institutes of higher learning in India, nearly 80 universities have introduced these subjects either at the under-graduate or at the post-graduate level or at both. Of these, nearly 60 universities have full-fledged departments of post-graduate teaching and research in sociology. In addition to these, some institutions of national importance, such as Indian Institutes of Technology at Delhi, Madras, Kanpur, Bombay and Kharagpur, Indian Institutes of Management at Bangalore, Calcutta and Ahmedabad, various regional engineering colleges and agricultural universities have also introduced teaching of sociology for the benefit of students in professional courses.

Apart from the full-fledged university departments, several constituent colleges within the jurisdiction of universities have introduced teaching in sociology at the under-graduate and post-graduate levels. To cite only a few examples, in Madhya Pradesh, 50 colleges affiliated to universities in the state teach sociology; of these, 11 colleges have post-graduate classes. In Uttar Pradesh, 127 colleges teach sociology at the under-graduate level and 27 of these do so either at post-graduate level only or at both under-graduate and post-graduate levels (UGC, 1979: 80-83). It is interesting to note that the expansion of sociology teaching has been considerable in relatively less developed states like Uttar Pradesh, Madhya Pradesh, Rajasthan, and Bihar. The growth is not as striking in more developed states like Punjab, Maharashtra, Gujarat, Karnataka, and Tamil Nadu. A possible explanation could be that the largest expansion is largely in the Hindi speaking belt where text-books in vernacular, of both good and bad quality, are available. Of course, expansion of sociology is catching up elsewhere, more impressively in Gujarat where again special attention has been paid by the government and the profession to the production of good text-books and reading material in the vernacular.

Student registration in sociology nearly equals that in economics, politics, and history and it certainly exceeds registration in other disciplines in the arts, humanities and social science faculties. This kind of expansion is conspicuously absent in social anthropology. Not more than a dozen universities can be counted where the teaching of anthropology is introduced at under-graduate and post-graduate levels. Similarly, anthropology curricula include courses on prehistory, archaeology, physical anthropology in addition to compulsory field-work and laboratory work. These have tended to restrict the number of students taking anthropology courses.

Certain trends in teaching are discernible. To make sociology and social anthropology more serviceable, compulsory courses on 'research methodology' and 'social statistics' have been introduced in the sociology and anthropology course-structures in several universities (UGC, 1979: 40-45, 89-93, 217-30, 240-41). The other important trend is to design courses so as to provide orientation in studying the structure of Indian society, social institutions, and dynamics. At the under-graduate level, importance is generally attached to introducing basic concepts in sociology and social anthropology and classical social thought. At the post-graduate level, however, more intensive studies in sociological theories and in some classics have been introduced besides compulsory methodology courses. In addition to these, a great variety of other courses and specializations are made available in rural, urban and industrial sociologies, social stratification and change, sociology of economic development, modernization, sociology of deviance, agrarian structure and change, sociology of education, and political sociology. More recently, courses on 'sociology of weaker sections' (i.e., Scheduled Castes, Scheduled Tribes and Backward Classes) have also been introduced in some universities. About two decades ago, courses on 'Introduction to Social Anthropology', 'Social Psychology' and 'Contemporary Social Problems' figured more commonly in sociology syllabi. These only showed the affinity of sociology to either social work or social anthropology. Very few places have still retained these as parts of sociology course-structure. The general tendency today is to replace them by courses on the growing frontiers of the disciplines like medical sociology, sociology of professions, sociology of law, sociology of science, sociology of mass communications, sociology of development, sociology of social movements and the like.

Research: incentives, promotion, publication, utilization, indigenization

Until 1950 or so, teaching was the principal activity of the professional sociologists and social anthropologists, who were based mostly in universities or colleges. Research activities were left to individual interests and initiatives. Government agencies rarely financed research in the universities and funds for research in the universities or colleges were scarce. Since the early 1950s, research activity has not only become an integral part of professional sociology and social anthropology but has also been recognized and rewarded. Those with higher research output and publications stand a better chance of promotions in the academic hierarchy.

Initially, funds for research came from government agencies like the UGC, Planning Commission and ICSSR. Even now the majority of research grants, funds for seminars, symposia or workshops and summer-institutes come either from the UGC or ICSSR. However, research funds for sociology and social anthropology have also come from industry, business, private charities, trusts and endowments etc. A special mention must be made here of the role of the Indian Council of Social Science

Research in promoting research in sociology and social anthropology. During the past twelve years of its existence the Council has sponsored hundreds of research projects initiated not only by sociologists and social anthropologists but also by other social scientists. The Council has offered grants for the publication of theses, for travelling abroad to collect useful material, and for study or lecture-tours. It offers fellowships to senior and junior members of the profession to undertake the research work of their choice. The Council has also established its own Data Archives and a Social Science Documentation Centre to provide assistance to researchers in data analysis as well as in bibliographic work. To facilitate communication of research results, the Council has also begun to publish abstracts of dissertations in sociology and social anthropology. The Council's quarterly *Newsletter* has also become an effective medium of communication in professional circles. The ICSSR's grants for research projects have been a welcome relief to several innovative and enterprising sociologists and social anthropologists. But, its policies, procedures and priorities leave much to be desired. First of all, ICSSR functions more as an extension of the Central Secretariat than as an "establishment of social scientists". Hence, red-tapism and bureaucratic delays in processing or reviewing project proposals are quite common. Secondly, ICSSR, at least initially, favoured survey type research proposals which was evident in the type of proforma it used for considering proposals. This resulted in the neglect of potentially good proposals based on library sources or secondary data. Thirdly, complaints are sometimes heard that research proposals are reviewed not necessarily by experts in the field concerned and that professional jealousies and rivalries have prevented the acceptance of potentially sound research proposals. Having fixed research priorities in the areas of 'weaker sections' or 'women studies', the ICSSR also tends to be too liberal in funding such projects. Consequently, although many project-reports are submitted to the ICSSR, very few of them deserve to be published. Some of these problems came up before the second review committee on ICSSR headed by V.M. Dandekar.

Research reports in the form of books are published mostly by private publishers. In the beginning, universities used to publish reports of the research projects approved or funded by them. Sometimes universities published manuscripts of invited lectures in the form of 'lecture-series'. At Calcutta, Bombay and other universities such publications came out at regular intervals. Research journals of universities were another important channel of communication. Because of financial difficulties, however, many universities have either suspended or drastically cut their publication programmes. One of the difficulties they faced was that the books or monographs published by them remained unsold for decades. Since universities were not commercially-oriented and had no sales network of their own, research publications gradually fell into the hands of private publishers who have flourished in India.

The utilization of sociology and social anthropology research leaves much to be desired. There are only two categories of consumers of the research output: professional sociologists and social anthropologists themselves who use research findings of others either for teaching purposes, for launching further research or for testing certain hypotheses at different levels. This kind of utilization has certainly increased during the last twenty years or so and has ensured a more sustained, systematic and cumulative growth of sociological knowledge in India. The other main consumer of research in the two disciplines is the government and its manifold agencies. Where research projects are sponsored by these agencies, the findings of the projects are evaluated and used for specific policy formulation or action programmes. The series of ICSSR projects on the Scheduled Castes in different regions could be cited as an example in recent years.

Professional organization

There are two main professional bodies of sociologists and social anthropologists. The Indian Sociological Society, founded in Bombay in the early 1950s, is an officially recognized organization.

On September 30, 1980 it had about 752 life members.* It publishes its own journal—*Sociological Bulletin* (29th Volume in 1980) and articles published in it are regularly abstracted in the *Sociological Abstracts*. All India Sociological Conferences are organized by the Society bi-annually and these have provided a forum for professional sociologists not only to exchange their views and research notes, but also to discuss problems faced by the profession (Atal, 1971: 431-33). The Indian Sociological Society has a fairly large number of professional social anthropologists among its life members. The other body is the Ethnographic and Folk Culture Society established by D.N. Majumdar in 1947 at Lucknow. It regularly publishes a quarterly journal—*Eastern Anthropologist*—which is a periodical recognized by international standards. There is also the Indian Anthropological Association, created by L.P. Vidyarthi and others. It publishes a separate periodical—*Indian Anthropologist*.

The growth of the profession has necessitated the formation of regional bodies of sociologists and social anthropologists in India. Such organizations, particularly in Uttar Pradesh, Rajasthan, Madhya Pradesh, Bihar, Karnataka and Kerala have been active. They have convened meetings and conferences occasionally and have affiliated themselves to the all-India bodies. The Indian Sociological Society is a member of the International Sociological Association.

Some sociologists and social anthropologists based in university departments, colleges and some research institutions, have also launched a number of research journals. Prominent among them are *Contributions to Indian Sociology* (New Series) edited by T.N. Madan; *Social Change* published by the Council for Social Development, New Delhi; *Indian Journal of Social Work*, published by the Tata Institute of Social Sciences, Bombay; *Social Action*, published by the Indian Social Institute, New Delhi, *Man in India*, founded by S.C. Roy in 1921 and now edited by Surjit Sinha.

---

* In September 1991 the total number of the Society's life members had reached 1397 (plus 137 foreign life members). See, *Sociological Bulletin*, Vol. 40, No. 1-2.

Among the other enterprises in research journal publications are *International Journal of Critical Sociology* (Jaipur), edited by T.K.N. Unnithan; *Indian Journal of Comparative Sociology* (Hyderabad), edited by C. Laxmanna; *Indian Journal of Social Research* (Baraut), edited by G.C. Hallen; *Kerala Sociologists*—a biannual journal published by the Kerala Sociological Society*; and *Emergent Sociology* (Meerut), edited by Brij Raj Chauhan. Besides these, periodicals like the *Indian Economic and Social History Review* (Delhi), *Economic and Political Weekly* (Bombay), *Journal of Social and Economic Studies* (A.N. Sinha Institute, Patna), *Social Scientist* (Indian School of Social Sciences, Trivandrum), and also *Indian Journal of Industrial Relations* (Shri Ram Institute, New Delhi), have also responded to inter-disciplinary and multi-disciplinary interests and have become very important for sociologists and social anthropologists in India.

Two problems concerning publication of these periodicals must be mentioned here. First, with the growing quantity, it has become increasingly difficult for editors to maintain quality. There are, of course, notable exceptions to this, but, in general, the pressure of quantity leading to deterioration of quality is being increasingly felt. Secondly, crisis and fluctuations in the printing industry, resulting from steadily rising costs have made it difficult to sustain regularity of publication of research journals. The ICSSR does provide financial assistance to some periodicals but it is not adequate to meet the rising costs.

International co-operation

Indian sociologists and social anthropologists have substantially benefited from collaborative and exchange programmes with foreign universites and governments. Fulbright and visiting fellowships offered by the American, British and other governments made it possible for several scholars to go abroad for further study, or on lecture-tours. Research projects have also been launched through

* *The Journal of Sociological Studies* (Jodhpur)—an annual edited by Sheo Kumar Lal, *Guru Nanak Journal of Sociology* (Amritsar) edited by Jaspal Singh.

collaborative efforts. Funds for these came either from foreign universities or from international aid agencies of the foreign governments. Particularly in the area of population studies, the Population Council made funds available. The Agricultural Development Council, World Bank, International Labour Organization and UNESCO too offered grants to Indian sociologists to undertake collaborative research in rural sociology, particularly on problems connected with rural development. Private endowments and foundations, like the Ford, Rockfeller, Nuffield, Rhodes and so on, have also provided funds to support fellowships to enable Indian scholars to travel abroad to attend seminars, conferences or to undertake study tours.

The Indian authorities frequently insist on screening proposals for such collaborative works and in that process delays become common. This is a major problem in international collaboration which needs to be tackled urgently.

Agenda for the future

Sociology and social anthropology in India are now mature social science disciplines. During the past sixty years of their professionalization and institutionalization, the two disciplines have acquired status and recognition which naturally raises hopes and expectations for them. What are the major lacunae in the disciplinary growth and how best could these be overcome so that the disciplines meet demands and challenges in future. The following suggestions and recommendations should answer these questions, at least partly if not wholly.

1. The focus of sociological inquiry in India has so far been on 'exploration and description'. Collection of facts, whether by direct observation or through secondary source material, is necessary but not sufficient to build a science. Moreover, for several years, Indian sociologists and social anthropologists showed only a limited interest in caste, tribe, kinship, village, marriage, and family. The very narrowness of these research concerns obviated the need for theory. Indian sociologists in some ways forestalled the need for theory by stereotyping the context of research

(Dhanagare, 1980: 25). It is true that the contexts of inquiry began to diversify after the 1950s. But, almost all the trend reports of ICSSR (1972-74) have revealed deficiencies in theory development. Systematic research, rooted in a theoretical framework and aimed at testing hypotheses, is lacking. The twin-disciplines must transcend 'description' and move from 'exploration' to 'explanation' or from 'what' and 'how' questions to 'why' questions.

2. Not that there is a total absence of theory in Indian sociology and social anthropology. Structural-functionalism was the dominant theoretical orientation until the early 1960s. Marxian, Weberian and Parsonian theoretic approaches too have been followed by some. At a somewhat lower level of abstraction and generalization, the framework of dominant caste and of Sanskritization has been fashionable. Incessant obsession with Sanskritization by several followers of Srinivas embarrassed even its author who confessed that he was bored with the concept (Srinivas, 1976: 2). Attempts to apply Weberian 'class, status, party' frame or concepts of 'bureaucracy' and 'charisma' too have been admirably made. Works within the framework of reference-group theory and more recently within the broad 'structuralist' framework are also noteworthy. Similarly, the use of Marxian theoretical approach based on dialectical and historical materialism is steadily increasing in Indian sociology. Although the awareness of theory and its importance in sociological research is growing, there is a tendency to apply theories almost mechanically. It needs to be stressed that creative interest in theory-building is lacking. The profession must reorient its teaching and research to generate such an interest.

3. An over-commitment to 'structural-functionalism' as a theoretical orientation has led to a near total immersion in the 'present'. The focus remained on the present structures of social relations and institutional arrangements. This gradually alienated the twin-disciplines from history. Obsession with 'present' structures resulted in the neglect of socio-historical perspective. True, some sociologists like D.P. Mukerji, Ramakrishna Mukherjee, A.R.

Desai, Yogendra Singh, Saberwal and Dhanagare used history meaningfully in their works. More recent are the writings of A.D. King (1976) and some social anthropologists such as R. Fox (1971), and Tom Kessinger (1974). But, there is a greater need to reorientate Indian sociology towards history. In recent studies on peasant resistance movements in India we see the younger generation of sociologists turning to social, political and economic history which enriches our understanding of the socio-cultural processes and the historical specificity of India's development experience (Dhanagare, 1980: 26).

4. At one stage, Indian sociologists were too anxious to participate in government policy formulation and evaluation. Serving the society by working for government and on its advisory or consulative bodies is, of course, a legitimate concern. But today, this has become only one of the several preoccupations of sociologists and social anthropologists. This is a healthy sign. Whether, as intellectuals, sociologists should be 'committed' or 'non-committed', and whether 'value-freeness' is possible or desirable are unresolved controversial questions. Individual members of the profession hold conflicting views and opinions. However, granting this, it can be stressed that one of the ways of serving the society is to develop sociology as social criticism as I have argued elsewhere (1980: 26).

5. The expanding profession requires ever-increasing financial resources. On this count there can be no complaint because social science in general, and sociology in particular, has received the best possible treatment, almost in excess of what it deserved, from UGC, ICSSR and other bodies. Resources made available for the growth of sociology and social anthropology have been more than adequate during the past two and half decades. A time has come when the profession must look back in retrospect, review its performance and above all learn to optimize utilization of the resources. There has to be a proper redistribution of resources as well. Initiatives in this regard must come from professional sociologists and social anthropologists who work as experts on numerous committees of the government, before bureaucrats begin

to give instructions about optimal utilization and redistribution.

6. Lastly, the dialectic of 'quantity' and 'quality' is, of course, inescapable. However, whether it is in teaching, in research, in theses evaluation or in publication, a relentless effort to maintain 'quality' is needed. No matter what specific area of interest one may pursue, it is ultimately the quality of academic excellence which will ensure a healthy growth of sociology and social anthropology in India.

References

Ahluwalia, A. 1974. 'Sociology of Medicine:A trend report', in ICSSR, *A Survey of Research in Sociology and Social Anthropology*,II, Bombay: Popular, pp. 401-30.

Alexander, K.C. 1968. *Social Mobility in Kerala*, Poona: Deccan Coolege Dissertation Series.

1975. *Agrarian Tension in Thanjavur*, Hyderabad: N.I.R.D.

Asad, T. (Ed.) 1973. *Anthropology and the Colonial Encounter*, London.

Atal, Yogesh 1968. 'The Role of Elites in Economic Development' (Seminar on Sociology of Economic Development) University of Saugar (mimeo). Later printed in *Indian Journal of Social Sciences* (Hyderabad), Vol. II, No. 122, 1972-73, pp.27-53.

1968. *The Changing Frontiers of Caste*, Delhi: National Publishing House.

1969. "Citizen's Sense of Political Efficacy", *Economic and Political Weekly* (Annual Number), January, pp. 171-78.

1971a. 'Professionalisation of Sociologists', *Economic and Political Weekly*, VI (6), pp. 431-33.

1971b. *Local Communities and National Politics*, Delhi: National Publishing House.

1976. *Social Sciences: The Indian Scene*, New Delhi: Abhinav Publications.

Balsara, J.F. 1964. *Problems of Rapid Urbanization in India*, Bombay: Popular Prakashan.

Baviskar, B.S. 1968. 'Union Politics and Management Politics", *Indian Journal of Industrial Relations*, 3 (3) pp. 300-315.

1969. 'Co-operatives and Castes in Maharashtra: A case study', *Sociological Bulletin*, 18 (2), pp. 148-67.

1974. 'Sociology of Politics: A trend report' in ICSSR, *A Survey of Research in Sociology and Social Anthropology*, II, Bombay: Popular Prakashan.

1980. *The Politics of Development: Sugar Cooperatives in Rural Maharashtra*, New Delhi: Oxford University Press.

Beteille, A. 1966. *Caste, Class and Power: Changing Patterns of Stratification in a Tanjore Village*, Berkeley: University of California Press.

1967. 'The Future of the Backward Classes', in P. Mason (ed.), *India and Ceylon: Unity and Diversity*, New York: Oxford University Press.

1969. *Castes: Old and New: Essays in Social Structure and Social Stratification*, Bombay: Asia Publishing House.

1973. 'Teaching of Sociology in India', *Sociological Bulletin*, 22 (2), pp. 216-33.

1974. *Studies in Agrarian Social Structure*, Delhi: Oxford University Press.

Bhat, A. 1970. 'Caste and Political Mobilization in a Gujarat District', in R. Kothari (Ed.), *Caste in Indian Politics*, Delhi: Orient Longman.

Bopegamage, A. 1955. *Delhi: A Study in Urban Sociology*, New Delhi: Longman Green.

Bose, A. 1970. *Urbanization in India*, Delhi: Academic Book Press.

Bose, N.K. 1968. *Calcutta—A Social Survey*, Bombay: Lalvani Publishing House.

Chakravarti, A. 1875. *Contradiction and Change: Emerging Patterns of Authority in a Rajasthan Village*, Delhi: Oxford University Press.

Chattopadhyaya, G. 1964. *Ranjana: A Village in West Bengal*, Calcutta: Book Land.

1969. 'Problem of Tribal Integration to Urban-Industrial Society', in *Economic and Political Weekly*, December 27, 1969 (with Baruna De).

Chattopadhyay, K.P. 1946. 'Economic Conditions of the Korkus of Melghat Forest', *Journal of the Royal Asiatic Society of Bengal*, 12 (1), pp. 43-70.

1947a. *Municipal Labour in Calcutta* (jointly with G.S. Ray), Calcutta: University of Calcutta.

1947b. *Report on the Santals in Northern and Western Bengal*, Calcutta: University of Calcutta.

1952. *A Socio-Economic Survey of the Jute Labour*, Calcutta: University of Calcutta.

Chauhan, B.R. 1967. *A Rajasthan Village*, New Delhi: Associated Publishing House.

1972. *Towns in Tribal Setting*, Delhi: National Publishing House.

1974. 'Rural studies-A trend report,' in ICSSR (1974), I, pp. 82-14.

Chitnis, S. 1969. 'The urban concentration of higher education', *Economic and Political Weekly* (July 1969), Special Number.

1974. 'Sociology of education:A trend report; in ICSSR (1974:II), pp. 166-216.

1977. A Long Way to Go: Report of a Survey of Scheduled Caste High School and College Students in 15 States in India, Bombay: Allied.

Damle, Y.B. 1955. *Communication of Modern Ideas and Knowledge in Indian Village*, Cambridge, M.I.T. Centre for International Relations.

1967. 'The School and College as a Social System', in M.S. Gore *et al* (Eds.), *Papers in Sociology of Education in India*, New Delhi: N.C.E.R.T., pp. 250-81.

1968. 'Reference group Theory with regard to Mobility in Caste', in J. Siverberg (Ed.), *Social Mobility in the Caste System in India*, The Hague: Mouton, pp. 95-102.

1970. 'Role of the Teacher in a Developing Society' in S.P. Ruhela (Ed.), *Sociology of the Teaching Profession in India*, New Delhi: N.C.E.R.T., pp. 169-175.

1971. 'Sociological Studies at the Deccan College', *Bulletin of the Deccan College Research Institute* (150th Anniversary Year Souvenir) , pp. 41-43.

Das, V. 1974. 'Sociology of Law:A trend report'; in ICSSR, *A Survey of Research in Sociology and Social Anthropology*, II, Bombay: Popular, pp. 367-400.

1977. *Structure and Cognition: Aspects of Hindu Caste and Ritual*, Delhi: Oxford University Press.

Desai, A.R. 1948. *Social Background of Indian Nationalism*, Bombay: Oxford University Press.

1961. *Rural India in Transition*, Bombay: Popular Prakashan.

1969. 'Introduction to rural sociology in India', in A.R. Desai (Ed.), *Rural Sociology in India*, Bombay: Oxford University Press.

Desai, A.R. (Ed.) 1979. *Peasant Struggles in India*, Bombay: Oxford University Press.

Desai, I.P. 1953. *High School Students in Poona*, Poona: Deccan College.

1956. 'Joint Family in India', *Sociological Bulletin*, 5 (2), pp. 144-56.
1964. *Some Aspects of Family in Mahuva*, Bombay: Asia.
1967. 'The Scope of a Sociology of Education' in M.S. Gore, I.P. Desai and Suma Chitnis (Eds.), *Papers in Sociology of Education in India*,. New Delhi: N.C.E.R.T., pp. 1-33.

Deva, I. 1953. *The Sociology of Bhojpuri Folk-Literature* (Ph.D. Disertation,Lucknow University).
1972. 'Folklore Studies:A trend report' in ICSSR, *A Survey of Research in Sociology and Social Anthropology*, III, Bombay: Popular Prakashan, pp. 197-239.

Dhanagare, D.N. 1974. 'Social Origins of the Peasant Insurrection in Telangana(1946-51)', *Contributions to Indian Sociology* (New Series), 8, pp. 109-34.
1975a, 'The Politics of Survival: Peasant Organizations and the Left-wing in India, 1925-46', *Sociological Bulletin*, 24 (I), pp. 29-54.
1975b. 'Congress and agrarian agitation in Oudh, 1920-22 and 1930', *South Asia* (5), pp. 67-77.
1976. 'Peasant, Protest and Politics: The Tebhaga Movement in Bengal (India) 1946-47', *The Journal of Peasant Studies*, III (3), pp. 360-78.
1977. 'Agrarian Conflict, Religion and Politics: the Moplah Rebellions in Malabar in the Nineteenth and Early Twentieth Centuries'. *Past and Present*, 74 (February, 1977), pp. 112-41.
1980. 'Search for Identity', *Seminar* (New Delhi), 254 (Studying our Society), October 1980, pp. 23-26.

D'Souza, V.S. 1968. *Social Structure of a Planned City—Chandigarh*, New Delhi: Orient Longmans Ltd.
1970. 'Slums and Social Structure', *Urban and Rural Planning Thought*, 8 (1-2), pp. 70-74.
1974, 'Urban Studies:A trend report', in ICSSR (1974) I, pp. 115-57.
1980. *Educational Inequalities among Scheduled Castes*, Occasional Monograph Series: 1, Chandigarh: University of Punjab, Department of Sociology.

Dube, Leela 1969. *Matriliny and Islam*, Delhi: National Publishing House.
1974. 'Sociology of Kinship: A trend report', in ICSSR, *A Survey of Research in Sociology and Social Anthropology*, Vol. II, Bombay: Popular Prakashan, pp. 233-366.

Dube, S.C. 1955. *Indian Village*, London: Routledge & Kegan Paul.

1958. *India's Changing Villages*, London: Routledge & Kegan Paul.

1964. 'Bureaucracy and Nation-Building in Transitional Societies', *International Social Science Journal*, 16 (2), pp. 229-36.

1966. 'Bureaucracy and Economic Development', *The Indian Journal of Public Administration*, 12 (3-), pp. 343-351.

1968. 'Caste Dominance and Factionalism', *Contributions to Indian Sociology* (New Series), No. 2 , December, pp. 58-81.

1969. 'Community Development: A critical review', in A.R. Desai (Ed.), *Rural Sociology in India*, Bombay: Popular Prakashan, pp. 622-26.

1974. 'Sociology of Economic Development:A trend report' in ICSSR, *A Survey of Research in Sociology and Social Anthropology*, II, Bombay: Popular Prakashan, pp. 1-29.

Dumont, L. 1970. *Homo Hierarchicus: The Caste System and its Implications*, Chicago: University Press.

Dutta, Ratna 1968. 'Values and Economic Development', *Economic and Political Weekly*, 3 (1-2), Annual Number, pp. 109-16.

1971. *Values in Models of Modernization*, Delhi: Vikas.

Ehrenfels, U.R. 1941. *Mother Right in India*, Oxford University Press.

Fox, R. 1971. *Kin, Clan, Raja and Rule: Hinterland Relations in Pre-Industrial India*, Bombay: Asia Publishing House.

Gaikwad, V.R. 1969. *Panchayati Raj and Bureaucracy*, Hyderabad: N.I.C.D.

Ghurye, G.S. 1938. 'Sex Habits of a Sample of Middle Class People of Bombay', in *Proceedings of the Second All India Population and the First Family Hygiene Conference*, Bombay: Karnataka Publishing House.

1943. *The Aborigines—'So Called'—and Their Future*, Poona: Gokhale Institute of Politics and Economics.

1962. *Family and Kin in Indo-European Culture*, Bombay: Popular Prakashan.

1963a. The Scheduled Tribes, Bombay: Popular Prakashan.

1963b. The Mahadev Kolis, Bombay: Popular Prakashan.

1964. Indian Sadhus, Bombay: Popular Prakashan.

1965. Religious Consciousness, Bombay: Popular Prakashan.

1968. Social Tensions in India, Bombay: Popular Prakashan.

1069. Caste and Race in India, Bombay: Popular Prakashan.

1972. Two Brahmanical Institutions: Gotra and Charan, Bombay: Popular Prakashan.

1973. *I and Other Explorations*, Bombay: Popular Prakashan.

Gore, M.S. 1965. 'The Crisis in University Education', in T.K.N. Unnithan *et al* (Eds.), *Towards a Sociology of Culture in India*, New Delhi: Prentice Hall (India), pp. 339-52.

1967. 'Sociology and Educational Research', in M.S. Gore *et al* (Eds.), *Papers in Sociology of Education in India*, New Delhi: N.C.E.R.T., pp. 335-56.

1968. *Urbanization and Family Change*, Bombay: Popular Prakashan.

Gough, K. (Ed.) 1961. *Matrilineal Kinship* (edited jointly with D.M. Schneider), Berkeley: University of California Press.

1966. 'Anthropology: Child of Imperialism', *Monthly Review*, 19(11), pp. 12-27.

1975. *Towards an Anthropology*, London: Monthly Review press.

Gupta, Surendra K. 1975. *Citizen in the Making*, Delhi: National Publishing House.

Haldipur, R.N. 1974. 'Sociology of Community Development and Panchayati Raj (Part I and II) in ICSSR, *A Survey of Research in Sociology and Social Arthropology*, II, Bombay: Popular Prakashan, pp. 30-165.

ICSSR. 1974. *A Survey of Research in Sociology and Social Anthropology* (in three volumes: Vol. III appeared first in 1972), Bombay: Popular.

Ishwaran, K. 1967. *Shivapur: A South Indian Village*, London: Routledge & Kegan Paul.

Joshi, P.C. 1968. 'Economic Development and the Indian Elite', *Link*, (January 26).

1969. 'Agrarian Social Structure and Social Change', *Sankhya-The Indian Journal of Statistics*, B31 (3-4), pp. 479-90.

1975. *Land Reforms in India*, New Delhi: Allied Publishers.

Kapadia, K.M. (Ed.) 1954. *Professor Ghurye Felicitation Volume*, Bombay: Popular Book Depot.

1955. *Marriage and Family in India*, Bombay: Oxford University Press.

1956. 'Rural Family Patterns-A study in Urban-Rural Relations' *Sociological Bulletin*, 5 (2), pp. 111-126.

1959. 'The Family in Transition', *Sociological Bulletin*, 8 (2), pp. 68-99.

Karve, I. 1953. *Kinship Organization in India* (first edition), Poona: Deccan College.

1961. *Hindu Society-An Interpretation*, Poona: Deccan College.

Kessinger, Tom G. 1974. *Vilayatpur 1848-1968:Social and Economic Change in a North Indian Village*, Berkeley: California University Press.

Khare, R.S. 1970. *The Changing Brahmans*, Chicago: The University of Chicago Press.

King, A.D. 1976. *Colonial Urban Development: Culture, Social Power and Environment*, London: Routledge & Kegan Paul.

Kothari, R. 1970a. *Politics in India*, Delhi: Orient Longman.

1970b. *Caste in Indian Politics*, Delhi: Orient Longman.

Lal, S.K. 1974. *The Urban Elite*, Delhi: Thomson Press (India).

Lal, S.K. 1974. and U.R. Nahar 1978. *Higher Education: Scheduled Castes and Scheduled Tribes*, Jodhpur: Jainsons.

Lambert, Richard D. 1963. *Workers, Factories, and Social Change in India*, Poona: Asia Publishing House and Gokhale Institute of Politics and Economics.

Madan, T.N. 1965. 'Structural Implications of Marriage in North India: Wife-Givers and Wife-Takers, among the Pandits of Kashmir', *Contributions to Indian Sociology*, 9 (2).

1977. 'Dialectics of Tradition and Modernity in the Sociology of D.P. Mukerji', *Sociological Bulletin*, 26 (2), September, pp. 155-78.

Majumdar, D.N. 1955. *Rural Profiles*, Lucknow: Ethnographic and Folk Culture Society.

1958. *Caste and Communication in an Indian Village*, Bombay: Asia Publishing House.

1960. *Social Contours of an Industrial City: Social Survey of Kanpur 1954-55*, Bombay; Asia Publishing House.

Malhotra, K.C. 1971. 'Anthropological Studies at the Deccan College', *Bulletin of the Deccan College Research Institute* (150th Anniversary Year-Souvenir), pp. 26-40.

Marriott, M. (Ed.)1955. *Village India: Studies in the Little Community*, Chicago: The University of Chicago Press.

Mathur, K.S. 1964. *Caste and Ritual in a Malwa Village*, Bombay: Asia Publishing House.

Mencher, J. 1978. *Agricultural and Social Structure in Tamil Nadu: Past Orgins, Present Transformation and Future Prospects*, New Delhi: Allied Publishers.

Mitra, A. 1967. 'A Functional Classification of India's Towns', in A. Bose (Ed.), *Patterns of Population Change in India 1951-61*, Calcutta:

Allied Publishers.

Moore, Jr., B. 1969. *Social Origins of Dictatorship and Democracy—Lord and Peasant in the Making of Modern World*: Penguine Books.

Mukherjee, R.K. 1926. *The Rural Economy of India*, London: Longman, Green & Co.

1927. *The Land Problems of India*, London: Longman, Green & Co.

1929. *Fields and Farmers of Oudh* (University of Lucknow: Studies in Economics and Sociology) Calcutta: Longman, Green & Co.

1931. 'Sociology and Mysticism', *Sociology and Social Research*, 15 (4), 303-10.

1938. 'The Sociological Analysis and Forecast of Population Increase', P*residential Address*: Second All India Population and First Family Hygiene Conference, Bombay: Karnataka Publishing House.

1945. *The Indian Working Class*, Bombay: Hind Kitab.

1949. *The Social Structure of Values*, London: Macmillan.

1951. *Inter-Caste Tensions* (with others), Lucknow: University of Lucknow (Mimeo).

1952. *A City in Transition: A Survey of Social Problems of Lucknow*, Lucknow: University of Lucknow.

1956. 'A General Theory of Society', in Singh, B. (Ed.), *The Frontiers of Social Science*, London: Macmillan & Co.

1963. *Social Profiles of a Metropolis: A Social and Economic Survey of Lucknow*, Bombay; Asia Publishing House.

1964. *A District Town in Transition: Social and Economic Survey of Gorakhpur* (with B. Singh), Bombay: Asia Publishing House.

1965. *The Oneness of Mankind*, London: Macmillan.

Mukerji, D.P. 1948. *Modern Indian Culture*, Bombay: Hind Kitab.

1958. *Diversities: Essays in Economics, Sociology and other Social Problems*, New Delhi: People's Publishing House.

Mukherjee, P.N. 1977. 'Social Movement and Social Change: Towards a Conceptual Clarification and Theoretic Orientation', *Sociological Bulletin*, 26 (I), pp. 38-59.

1978. 'Naxalite Movement and Peasant Revolt in North Bengal', in M.S.A. Rao (Ed.), *Social Movements in India*, I, New Delhi: Manohar, pp. 17-90.

Mukherjee, Ramakrishna 1949. 'The Economic Structure and Social Life in Six Villages of Bengal', *American Sociological Review*, 14 (3), pp. 415-25.

1975. *The Dynamics of a Rural Society*, Berlin: Akademie-Verlag.

1958. *Six Villages of Bengal*, Bombay: Popular Prakashan (new edition).

1977a. *West Bengal Family Structures: 1946-66*, Delhi: Macmillan Co.

1977b. 'Trends in Indian sociology,' *Current Sociology*, 25 (3), pp. 1-193.

Nisbet, R.A. 1966. *The Sociological Tradition*, New York: Basic Books.

Oommen, T.K. 1970. 'The Concept of Dominant Caste: some queries', *Contributions to Indian Sociology* (New Series No. 4), December, pp. 73-83.

1972. *Charisma, Stability and Change*, New Delhi: Thomson.

1975. 'Agrarian Legislations and Movements as Sources of Social Change', *Economic and Political Weekly*, 10 (40).

1977. 'From Mobilization to Institutionalization: The Life Cycle of an Agricultural Labour Movement in Kerala' in S.C. Malik (ed.), *Dissent, Protest and Reforms in Indian Civilization*, Simla: Indian Institute of Advanced Study.

Pandey S.M. 1967. 'Rival Unionism in an Industrial Centre', *Indian Journal of Industrial Relations*, 3 (2), pp. 138-59.

1968. 'Ideological Conflict in the Kanpur Trade Union Movement', *Indian Journal of Industrial Relations*, 3 (3), pp. 243-68.

Parvathamma, C. 1964. 'Elections and Traditional Leadership in a Mysore Village', *Economic and Political Weekly*, 17 (10 & 11), pp. 475-81, 511-18.

1968. 'Landholding Pattern and Power Relations in a Mysore village' *Sociological Bulletin*, 17 (2), pp. 203-24.

Patwardhan, S. 1968. 'Social Mobility and Conversion of Mahars', *Sociological Bulletin*, 17 (2), pp. 187-222.

Pimpley, P.N. 1980. *A Profile of Scheduled Castes Students: The Case of Punjab* (Occasional Monograph Series: 2) Chandigarh: University of Punjab-Department of Sociology.

Punekar, S.D. 1948. *Trade Unionism in India*, Bombay: New Book Co.

1967. *Trade Union Leadership in India* (with S. Madhuri), Bombay: Lalvani.

Rajgopalan, C. 1960. 'Bombay: A Study in Urban Demography and Ecology', *Sociological Bulletin*, 9 (I), pp. 16-33.

1962. *The Greater Bombay*, Bombay: Popular Book Depot.

Ramaswamy, E.A. 1969. 'Trade Unions and Politics', *Sociological*

Bulletin, 18 (2), pp. 133-48.
1977. *The Worker and His Union*, New Delhi: Allied.

Rao, M.S.A. 1968. 'Political Elite and Caste Association', *Economic and Political Weekly*, May 18, pp. 779-82.
1969. 'Religion and Economic Development', *Sociological Bulletin*, 18(I), pp. 1-5.
1970. *Urbanization and Social Change*, New Delhi: Orient Longman.
1974, 'Introduction' to a *Survey of Research in Sociology and Social Anthropology*, Vol. I, ICCSR.
1978. *Social Movements in India(Vol. I)*, New Delhi: Manohar and *Vol. II* in (1979).
1979a. *Social Movements and Social Transformation: A Study of Two Backward Classes Movements in India*, New Delhi: Macmillan.
1979b, 'Sociology in the 1980's, *Economic and Political Weekly*, XIV (44), November 3, pp. 1810-1815.

Rastogi, P.N. 1964. 'Factionalism, Politics and Crime in a U.P. village', *Eastern Anthropologists*, 17(2) pp. 168-82.
1967. 'Anatomy of Factional Conflict', *Sociological Bulletin*, 16(I), pp. 17-32.
1973. 'Structure, Function and Process: A Cybernetic Approach to Social Phenomena', *Sociological Bulletin*, 22(2), pp. 309-320.
1975. *The Nature and Dynamics of Factional Conflicts*, New Delhi: Macmillan.

Saberwal, S. 1976. *Mobile Men: Limits to Social Change in Urban Punjab.*, Delhi: Vikas Publishing House.
1977. 'Status and Entrepreneurship: The Ramgarhia Case', in M.N. Srinivas *et al* (eds.), *Dimensions of Social Change in India*, Bombay: Allied Publishers.

Schchidananda, 1964. *Culture Change in Tribal Bihar*, Calcutta: Bookland Pvt. Ltd.
1968. *The Tribal Village in Bihar: A Study in Unity and Extension*, New Delhi: Oriental Publishers.
1974. 'Research on Scheduled Castes with reference to Change: A trend report', in ICSSR (1974), pp. 276-310.
1977. *The Harijan Elite: A Study of their Status, Networks, Mobility and Role in Social Transformation*, Delhi: Thomson Press (India) Ltd.

Sakesena, R.N. 1964. *Sociology and Social Policy in India*, Calcutta:

Orient Longmans.

Saran, A.K. 1958. 'India' in Roucek J.S. (Ed.), *Contemporary Sociology*, New York: Philosophical Library, pp. 122-35.

1962a. 'For a Sociology of India', *EasternAnthropologists*, 15(I), pp. 53-68.

1962b. 'Hinduism and Economic Development in India', *Archieves de Sociologie des Religions*, pp. 8-15.

1968. 'The Concept of Social Science', in Sharma, K.D. (Ed.), *Basic Issues in Social Sciences*, Bombay: Academic Journals of India, pp. 17-49.

Shah, A.M. 1964. 'Basic Terms and Concept in the Study of Family in India' *Indian Economic and Social History Review*, 1(3), pp. 1-36.

1968. 'Change in the Indian Family', *Economic and Political Weekly*, 3 (1 & 2), pp. 127-35.

1973. *The Household Dimension of the Family in India*, Delhi: Orient Longmans.

Shah, B.V. 1960. 'Inequalities in Educational Opportunities, *Economic and Political Weekly*, 12(34).

1965. 'Sociology of Education: An Attempt at Definition and Scope', *Sociological Bulletin*, 14(2).

1968. 'Student Unrest: A Sociological Hypothesis', *Sociological Bulletin*, 17 (I), pp. 55-64.

Sharma, K.L. 1970. 'Caste and Class Consciousness in Rural Rajasthan', *Sociology and Social Research*, 54(3), pp 278-87.

1974 *The Changing Rural Stratification System*, New Delhi: Orient Longman.

Sharma, K.L. 1975. *Entrepreneurial Performance in Role Perspective*, Delhi: Abhinava Publications.

1978. 'A Multi-Variate Model for the Analysis of Entrepreneurship in Manufacturing Organization', *Sociological Bulletin*, 27(I) March, pp. 48-67.

Sheth, N.R. 1968. *The Social Framework of an Indian Factory*, Bombay: Oxford University Press.

1974. 'Industrial Sociology:A trend report', in ICSSR, *A Survey of Research in Sociology and Social Anthropology*, Vol. II, Bombay: Popular Prakashan, pp. 158-179.

Singh, R. 1974. 'Agrarian Social Structure and Peasant Unrest: A Study of Landgrab Movement in District Basti, East U.P.', *Sociological Bulletin*, 23(I), pp. 44-70.

1978. 'Peasant Movement in Uttar Pradesh', in M.S.A. Rao (Ed.), *Social Movements in India*, I, New Delhi: Manohar, pp. 91-148.

Singh, Yogendra 1969a. 'Changing Power Structure of Village Community' in A.R. Desai (Ed.), *Rural Sociology in India*, Bombay: Popular Prakashan.

1969b. 'Social Structure and Village Panchayats: A Case Study in Class Relations in Rural Political Process', in M.V. Mathur and I. Narain (eds.), *Panchayati Raj, Planning and Democracy*; Bombay: Asia, pp. 352-64.

1973. *Modernization of Indian Tradition*, Delhi: Thomson Press (India) Ltd.

1977. 'Theory, Ideology and Methods in Indian sociology' (A review of a quarter of a century 1952-77) a paper prepared for UNESCO Round Table, Paris (21-25 October, 1977) (Mimeographed).

Singhi, N.K. 1974, *Bureaucracy Positions and Persons: Role Structures, Interactions and Value Orientations of Bureaucrats in Rajasthan*, New Delhi: Abhinav.

1979. *Education and Social Change*, Jaipur: Rawat.

Sinha, S. 1974. 'Sociology of religion:A trend report', in ICSSR, *A Survey of Research in Sociology and Social Anthropology*, II, Bombay: Popular, pp. 508-30.

Sirsikar, V.M. 1970. *The Rural Elite in a Developing Society: A Study in Political Sociology*, New Delhi: Orient Longman.

Sovani, N.V. 1966. *Urbanization and Urban India*, Bombay: Asia Publishing House.

Srinivas, M.N. 1942. *Marriage and Family in Mysore*, Bombay: New Book Co.

1952. *Religion and Society among the Coorgs of South India*, Oxford: Claredon Press.

1959. 'The Dominant Caste in Rampura', *American Anthropologist*, 61(I), pp. 1-16.

1960. *India's Village*, Bombay: Asia Publishing House.

1962. *Caste in Modern India and other Essays*, Bombay: Asia Publishing House.

1966. *Social Change in Modern India*, Bombay: Allied Publishers.

1971. 'Obituary: Professor A.R. Wadia, 1888-1971', *Sociological Bulletin*, 20(2), pp. 202-205.

1976. 'Rural India through a Microscope' (interviewed by H. Kusumakari). *The Times of India (Sunday Magazine)*, June 6, 1976.

p. 2

1977. *The Remembered Village*, New Delhi: Oxford University Press.

Srinivas, M.N., Y.B. Damle, S. Shahani and A. Beteille 1959a. 'Caste: A Trend Report and Bibliography', *Current Sociology*, 8(3), pp. 133-83.

Srinivas, M.N., and Panini, M.N. 1973. 'The Development of Sociology and Social Anthropology in India', *Sociological Bulletin*, 22(2), pp. 179-215.

Uberoi, J.P.S. 1974. 'New Outlines of Structural Sociology, 1845-1970', *Contributions to Indian Sociology* (New Series) No. 8, pp. 135-52.

1978. *Science and Culture*, New Delhi: Oxford University Press.

University Grants Commission. 1979. *Report on the Status of Teaching of Sociology and Social Anthropology* (Part II), New Delhi, UGC.

Unnithan, T.K.N., Deva, I. and Singh, Y. (Eds.) 1965. *Towards a Sociology of Culture in India*, New Delhi: Prentice Hall.

Verma, S.C. 1979. 'Social inquiry for What?' in M. Mullick (Ed.), *Social Enquiry: Goals and Approaches*, New Delhi: Manohar.

Vidyarthi, L.P. 1967. 'Industrialization and its Social Consequences: Urbanization and Industrialization in India in general, and in the Chotanagpur region in particular' (unpublished).

1970. *Socio-Cultural Implications of Industrialisation in India: A Case Study of Tribal Bihar*, Delhi: R.P.C. Planning Commission.

Chapter four

Prospects of an integrated approach to social reality

The formulation 'social reality' involves intriguing questions in the sociology of knowledge, such as "what is real?", "how is one to know it?", and "how best the gap between 'reality' and its conceptual reconstruction in the process of knowing can be narrowed down?" Although the general tendency in the social sciences is to accept the concept of 'social reality' as a term whose meaning is deemed to be known to its users, Berger and Luckmann (1971) have made us aware of the deep philosophical and epistemological connotations of the words 'reality' and 'social reality'. Apart from these basic questions pertaining to 'reality' and 'knowledge' in which a sociologist should be no less interested than his colleagues in social philosophy, the problem of social relativity of 'reality' and the ultimate validity or invalidity of knowledge are equally vexing.

The present paper,[1] however, is not an attempt at discussing the meaning of 'social reality' in the framework of the sociology of knowledge. We shall, therefore, bypass the deep philosophical questions without under-rating their importance. Here we shall take 'social reality' as given—implying that society is an objective reality, although it may be differently perceived, conceived, and interpreted. We assume that it is possible to understand society—its basic structures and dynamics—through procedures of empirical observation and verification as well as through intuitive philosophical reflection. We treat these two methods of understanding as mutually complementary rather than contradictory. The ways of understanding society are manifold and those who seek to know it may not necessarily agree on the adequacy and the utility of a particular mode of understanding. It is with this broad positivist yet liberal conviction that this paper seeks to explore the possibilities of integrating alternative approaches to the understanding of social reality. Particularly our focus will be on the nature, the scope, and the limitations of what we call an 'integrated approach'. We shall also discuss later the status of theory and the role of social values in the context of our advocacy in favour of an integrated approach to the understanding of social reality.

Conceptions of society

There are two broad conceptions of society or of the relationship between man and society. One of these may broadly be called the 'emergent' conception which views society or social order as *sui generis*. Man's interrelationships with his environment, human or otherwise, produce institutions, norms of conduct, and all forms of typifications which imply historicity and control. This conception, therefore, treats 'social order' as prior, as something that transcends the individuals who constitute it. Society is viewed as a natural boundary-maintaining system of all human actions. The lack of the transcendent nature of society is treated as equivalent of lack of social control—which means 'anomie' (Horton, 1966:705). The sociological tradition that subscribes to this emergent notion of society is often traced to Emile Durkheim (1964). The other may be termed as the 'immanent' conception which views 'social order' as basically a human product. It implies that society exists only as a product of human activity. Externalization is a fundamental biological need; and human beings have the necessary biological equipment to realize it. The so-called *sui generis* social order is thus reduced to the human individuals who constitute it. Thus, society or social world is conceived as nothing more than a summation of its constituents. The conflict theorists, for example, subscribed to the immanent conception and viewed society not as a transcendent social order but as a continually "contested struggle between groups and classes with opposing goals, perspectives and world-views" (Horton, 1966: 705-6). Karl Marx, for example, considered the transcendence of society as tantamount to alienation of man from his own social nature (Bottomore and Rubel, 1971: 102-14; 175-

85). Both these conceptions are somewhat 'ideal type' polarities that miss the fundamental dialectical nature of the relationship between human activity and experience on the one hand and the institutional order—that is, not only the product of human activity but also an objective reality in its own right, on the other. For our purpose, then, we may proceed with the following basic premises: (a) that society as a social reality is a human product; (b) that it is an objective reality that is independent of its components and one which is amenable to empirical verification and understanding; and (c) that man is a social product at the same time as society is viewed as a human product.[2]

The purpose of restating these familiar premises is to highlight the integral nature of man-society relationship, or of the relationship between man, nature, and society. The three are only abstractions and conceptualizations drawn from what is an extremely complex, and yet indivisible, set of inter-connections. This is not to suggest that the founding-fathers of modern social sciences in the late eighteenth century and in the nineteenth century were grossly unaware of this basically indivisible interrelationship between man, nature and society. Despite the fact that this awareness was often reflected in the writings of social philosophers of the pre-industrial era, attempts at studying man, in relation to nature and society, got compartmentalized into a host of specialized disciplines. These attempts eventually got institutionalized into independent scientific domains. Even a cursory look at the schemes of classification of 'sciences' in the writings of August Comte, Herbert Spencer down to Wilhelm Dilthey and Max Weber would reveal the underlying intellectual justifications for creating separate sciences—with peculiar sets of concepts and methodologies—which were meticulously sustained and preserved, though seldom advanced, by their disciples in the present-day social sciences.

Unity and duality of sciences

The intention here is not to deny the fundamental duality of sciences—a notion to which we subscribe. At the level of the spirit and ethic of scientific inquiry one could find a basic identity between the 'natural' and the 'humanistic or social' sciences. Philosophical evidence suggests that the method in the natural sciences is based on the same kind of cycles of interpretation as are commonly associated with social sciences (Kuhn, 1970). Empirical observations suggest that "natural science investigation is grounded in the same kind of situational logic and marked by the same kind of indexical reasoning which we are used to associate with the symbolic and interactional character of social systems or social world" (Knorr, 1977: 689- 96). However, more recently, methodological discussions have pointed out the essential inadequacies of the positivistic model for social science methodologies and have highlighted the significant differences between concrete method, analysis, and research procedures of the social sciences and those of the natural sciences (Knorr-Cetina, 1981: 335-36). Therefore, the two realms of sciences had to follow entirely different sets of logic of proof, of verification, and bases of generalizations in their development throughout the nineteenth century and thereafter. What is interesting is the fact that the compartmentalization did not stop at the simple binary division between 'natural' and 'social' sciences; the process of specialization by disciplines got proliferated not altogether without any purpose or justification.

Growth of sociology, psychology, anthropology, comparative religion and politics, and economics was mainly in the form of branching off from social philosophy which in its classical formulations had viewed the integral nature of social reality. The development of various specialized social science disciplines was in a large measure a response to the nature of transformation wrought about by the industrial capitalism throughout the nineteenth century. Elaborate division of labour based on high degree of specialization characterized the work organization in modern industrial societies. Advances in science and technology and their application to productive processes led to atomization and gradual fragmentation of the integral units of man-society relationship. Specialization in social sciences, emergence of a number of sub-disciplines, and a somewhat pathological keenness to demarcate boundaries of one science from the other were only manifestations of that fragmentation. The branching-off of various specialized social science disciplines and sub-disciplines may be viewed as the need of the time and yet it reflects the segmental view of man which this process encouraged. Specialization in modern society thus acts as a double-edged weapon. It ensures a high degree of expertise in a sector of learning, but at the same time it creates conditions of self-imposed isolation from other pursuits of learning. The latter typifies the present-day social science scene in our academies.

Interdisciplinary exchange: the natural versus social science experience

Before examining the scope and the potential for an integrated approach in the social sciences, it would be quite instructive to acquaint ourselves with the experience of the natural sciences. In this area there has been a more meaningful interaction among different disciplines over several centuries and their progress has been more orderly and better regulated. This is not to suggest that the natural sciences have reached the pinnacle of perfection and have solved all problems and riddles. But among the natural sciences there is a common trunk, going from mathematics to quantum mechanics, then to physics, from there to chemistry, biology, and from there even to physiological psychology. In other words, we can discern in the natural sciences a series of 'decreasing generality' and 'increasing complexity'. Using these classificatory criteria, which we have borrowed from Comte, we can certainly place various natural sciences in a hierarchical order where specialists in one would need collaboration of research workers belonging to the preceding sciences in a given order (Piaget, 1973: 9-10).

Thus, we find that physics finds mathematics indispensable, and theoretical physics, while lending itself to experimentation, is essentially mathematical in its form as well as in technique and application. Similarly, mathematicians are concerned with physics in that they, by deduction, solve certain problems posed by physics. A chemist cannot go very far without physics, and a biologist needs chemistry, physics, and mathematics. In all these fields, therefore, interdisciplinary research is becoming imperative for attempting the integration of perspectives and for enriching our understanding of the material world. It must, however, be stressed that such integration is facilitated by the nature of the subject-matter, and by a clearly defined order of disciplines, determined by the principles of decreasing generality and increasing complexity that find wider acceptance in the natural sciences. Consequently, a whole range of new sciences, such as biophysics, biochemistry, biometry, etc. are emerging with their increasing complexity.[3]

In the field of human sciences, interdisciplinary research can result from two separate but interrelated needs. First is the 'need for information' and more data, and the second is the need for more common structures or for analytical integration. At the first level, an interdisciplinary collaboration poses little or no problems. It involves exchange of information among related disciplines in the belief that such exchange enriches a discipline's understanding of the phenomena under study. A discipline's boundaries and autonomy in explanatory terms are not eroded by interdisciplinary contacts at the level of information or data. It may sometimes lead to adoption of common methods by related disciplines, which in turn, may pave the way for a possible integration at the level of analysis or perspectives or interpretative scheme. The fulfilment of this second need for common structures, or what we have termed as analytical integration, is beset with several difficulties. Unlike in the natural sciences, in the social sciences there is no linear order of sciences ranged between 'decreasing generality' and 'increasing complexity'. On the contrary, in some of the social sciences, there is a marked tendency to reduce explanations of diverse social phenomena to a single perspective peculiar to that science. Sociologists are often accused of reducing everything to sociology and their reductionism is often pejoratively dubbed as 'sociological imperialism'. Similar tendencies are noticeable, with differences in degree, among some economists, political scientists, linguists, psychologists, and so on. In our opinion, the challenges posed by reduction, particularly in the social sciences, to some extent explain the growing interdisciplinary trend that is receiving a continual impetus today. Consequently, like in the natural sciences, even in the field of social sciences a whole range of 'new specializations' are emerging and we have 'sociolinguistics', 'political sociology', and 'economic anthropology' (Godelier, 1976), and the like. These are, in turn, paving the way for an integrated approach in the field of social sciences.

Implicit in our argument is integration of perspectives, i.e., analytical integration, which is possible by synthesizing theoretical formulations and empirical findings produced across social science disciplines. This is possible by what Piaget (1973: 11) has called 'reciprocal assimilation', by partial reduction of the 'higher', but also by enrichment of the 'lower' by the 'higher'. Going over the bounds of one's own discipline at the analytical level implies a synthesis of perspectives, and an assimilation of scientific explanations. Such convergence is warranted more by the nature of social facts or social phenomena that social scientists deal with. For such a convergence, social scientists must begin by comparing their problems first; if there is convergence of certain general problems, then they must see whether the two sets of problems and social realities they deal with have connections with other areas that are dealt with by other disciplines; and finally, to solve those problems, they must examine whether it is necessary to take recourse to any seminal ideas which actually rest on common mechanisms, or on integrated, synthesized analytical scheme.

Status of theory in integrated approach

Fortunately, the logic and the structure of certain social theories and perspectives are conducive to such an integration. But neither have their explanatory powers been fully tapped nor are their adaptive and innovative potentialities sufficiently revealed so far. Reference may be made here to the Marxian general theory of history, particularly 'dialectical materialism', Talcott Parsons' theory of social systems (1970: 3-23) and action frame of reference (1977: 43-51, 731-57), and also to more recent advances made in structuralism. This is only by way of illustration and not an exhaustive list of perspectives which we consider as inherently facilitating synthesis.[4] Functionalism and structural-functionalism in anthropology too had this potential for synthesis. However, in the hey-day of functionalism, 'structure' was used more as a static concept. Consequently, complex social processes tended to be reduced to simple mechanistic formulae—mostly derived from analogies and isomorphism with biological systems. Later, and at a higher level of abstraction, in the systemic analytical framework this narrowness was overcome as 'structure' came to be viewed as having an inherently dynamic character and 'change' was seen as the result of 'structural differentiation'. This is not to suggest that systems theorists of analysis became less interested in the problems of systems maintenance and the *status quo*. Nevertheless, these developments paved the way for some dialogue between the adherents of the dialectical theoretical tradition and those of the systemic theoretical tradition. Such attempts to synthesize these two or more approaches for theoretic assimilation could be mentioned as one of the striking features of the European intellectual tradition today. Qualitative differences in their emphases still persist. For example, the systems approach continues to focus on functional equilibrium as 'homeostasis' whereas the dialecticians treat it as 'homeorhesis' or dialectical equilibrium as the essence of the process of structural transformation (Ball, 1979: 785-96). Althusserian attempts to combine the structuralist and Marxist perspectives are points in this direction of synthesis and assimilation at the theoretic level (Althusser and Balibar, 1970; Rex, 1974). Alan Touraine's (1977) work may also be cited as an important landmark in this context.

In India so far such an integration or theoretical synthesis is not in sight. Few social scientists demonstrate even the awareness of theory and those who recognize the relevance of theory for any systematic understanding of social phenomena are still fewer. Even where theory is taken seriously, as is the case of sociology in India, to confine to my own discipline, the systemic theoretical exercises have been made by Yogendra Singh (1973), Y.B. Damle (1965: 32-52; 1967: 250-81) and others, whereas the Marxian dialectical analyses have grown somewhat independently of the former (e.g.,

A.R. Desai, 1948; 1969). Even rudimentary efforts in the direction of synthesis or integration are lacking in India.

Basically all the theories only represent different alternatives of appraising social reality. But Ramkrishna Mukherjee notes some striking features of theoretical orientations in sociology. First, that these theoretical alternatives have a deductive-positivist base and that "there is no objective basis from which to infer their relative powers of explanation and prediction vis-a-vis the contextual reality". Instead, it is left to the subjective judgements of the proponents of the various theoretical alternatives. Therefore, although theories are mutually distinct, they, in effect, express both 'facts' and 'values'. Secondly, this undoubtedly influences the cause-and-effect ordering of facts in various theoretical alternatives. The ideological loads and differences among sociologists thus lead them to promote one or another alternative appraisal of social reality (Mukherjee, 1977: 33-34). As a reaction to this situation, Mukherjee prefers to come out of a vicious circle of an ideologically loaded deductive positivism and advocates what he calls an inductive-inferential approach to social reality. Two points could be raised on Mukherjee's proposed approach. First, he presumes that inductive sociological exercises will *not* demonstrate oppositional value preferences as deductive positivist alternatives do. Secondly, what kind of theoretical breakthrough will induction achieve? Mukherjee confesses that in the immediate future inductive-inferential approach will not achieve such a breakthrough (*ibid.*: 135). But, the contribution such an approach is likely to make either to the development of a new theory or integration of existing theories is not precisely spelled out by Mukherjee. In the absence of these, his views practically border on nihilism or an anti-theoretical position or both.[5]

At the level of theory,[6] to what model of theory should the protagonists of integrated approach subscribe? Here, monastic and pluralistic theoretical models provide us with two clear alternatives. Seen in the true spirit of integration the monastic theory model looks incompatible with the tasks of synthesis and assimilation which face the social scientists today. Such theories are possible only where scientists have succeeded in establishing causal explanations that facilitate predictions and control. The credit for having achieved these is often given to natural sciences but even there scepticism over the tenability of 'causal' (i.e., predictive) explanation is growing. In our opinion the nature as well as the objectives of 'social causation' is basically different from causation in the natural sciences. The goal of social science inquiry could at best be 'understanding' (implying Max Weber's exegesis—interpretation) or 'trend analysis' and not 'prediction' (Kaplan, 1964: 346-56). The nature of scientific explanation, and therefore of theory in humanistic sciences, is 'stochastic' or 'probabilistic'. Today even the natural scientists have a secular position. Various alternative explanations of social phenomena are possible. This leads us to a pluralist theoretical position. However, the tasks involved in integrated approach must not remain confined only to recognizing the plurality of the social forces that operate; they must also include evaluation of the relative importance of those social forces. An attempt must necessarily be made to indicate which of the interpretations is more tenable and which social forces prove to be more decisive in time and space. Social scientists have to tackle the problems of analysis at the 'synchronic' and the 'diachronic' levels. The real success of an integrated approach lies in explaining social reality at both the levels. Moreover, theoretical pluralism implies relativism which means that there need not be *the* theory, or *the* explanation for all times to come. What is relatively a more important and determining force at a particular phase in societal development may not always remain so in time and space. Hence, theoretical or analytical integration is not a one-time feat but an endless process that has to be kept up relentlessly.

Orientations in integrated approach

All those social scientists interested in studying social reality in an integrated and interdisciplinary perspective may have three possible alternative types of orientation, viz., cognitive, affective, and conative. Conventionally, cognitive orientation has been considered not only necessary but also desirable as an integral part of any scientific pursuit. The cognitive orientation itself operates at two levels. At one level it manifests itself through a description of the phenomenon which is being observed in terms of the concepts commonly used by diverse social science disciplines. Here similarities and differences in the conceptual connotations familiar in respective social science fields must first be carefully sorted out. This will ensure multifaceted descriptions that are mutually complementary and reinforcing. At the other level the cognitive orientation manifests in explanatory exercises. Scientific explanation is an attempt to answer 'why' and under 'what conditions' the phenomenon occurs and with 'what consequences' (Gore, 1976: 9-10). Most of the social sciences in the Anglo-American intellectual tradition have laid emphasis on these aspects of the cognitive orientation.

The other two orientations—affective and conative—have so far been considered as inappropriate for 'pure' scientists. The canons of positivism, of objectivity, and, more particularly, of ethical neutrality and value-free knowledge discouraged social scientists from adopting affective or even conative orientation towards social realities. These orientations denote psychological and affective involvement of a scientist and his will or desire that would ultimately reflect in social action. The controversy over 'value-free' and 'value-based' social science is age-old and yet an unresolved one. But there has been a marked shift in favour of the latter in more recent years (e.g., see Mullick, 1979). The role of value judgements in (a) the selection of problems, (b) the determination of the contents of conclusion, (c) the identification of facts, and (d) the interpretation and assessment of evidence is most vital. As Ernest Nagel has put it: "[the] social scientist selects what...[are] the socially important values; and he attributes 'cultural significance' so that value-orientation is inherent in his choice of material for investigation" (1961: 1-14). Thus, although Max Weber was a vigorous proponent of 'value-free social science', his contention nevertheless was that the concept of culture itself has a value-concept and an empirical reality became 'culture' to us as we related it to value-ideas. Thus, we cannot, and must not, discover what is meaningful to us by means of a 'presuppositionless' excursion into empirical data. Orthodox social scientists, however, continue to cling to 'value-neutrality' as the essence of science in methodological sense. To them affective orientation is by its very nature non-objective, and conative orientation presupposes certain prescriptive, normative concerns or 'end-states' in terms of which existing reality is sought to be evaluated, modified, and changed if necessary. Unfortunately, most social scientists today choose to accept the role of self-appointed guardians of objectivity and prefer to talk of 'social change' as if it were value-free.

Social scientists operating within an integrated frame have then two options. They may choose to refrain from prescriptive and 'end-state directed activities' and thus confine themselves to purely cognitive-type of scientific studies, whether descriptive or explanatory or both. Implicit in this position is an assumption that complete objectivity and value-free knowledge are possible. In such an ideally detached frame of analysis researchers function purely as technocrats and do not wish to, or pretend not to, be committed to any set of value preferences. Alternatively, social scientists can opt for a committed science in which research pursuits have social relevance and are anchored in certain end-states—whether directly or indirectly. Social reality would not only be understood but sought to be modified or changed in relation to value preferences. An interdisciplinary research team must be homogeneous in terms of its orientation. A team with some members trying to remain 'aloof and detached' and others with avowed commitment will not be a viable one because its members are likely to engage themselves in activities that pull them apart and can function at cross purposes.[7]

Our own preference is for a social science that is committed and is socially relevant.[8] This choice is dictated by two considerations. First, that absolute 'value-neutrality' is not possible except in the form of pure and simple abstraction or mental construct. Thus, 'value-freeness' borders on 'valuelessness'. Often value-choices tacitly influence scientific endeavours and still claims to 'scientific objectivity' are voiced most vociferously. This is far more dangerously misleading because in that case value-loads operate at the unconscious level under the facade of scientific objectivity. Therefore, the best course for social scientists is to make their value-preferences explicit, whatever they may be, and then try to conform to the rigours of scientific objectivity. In fact, "to be aware of one's own value-preferences itself is a step towards scientific objectivity" (Srinivas, 1970: 4-5). Secondly, in the methodology of social sciences, which is styled mostly on the model of natural sciences, unfortunately 'value-preference' and 'scientific objectivity' are pitted against each other as mutually incompatible polarities. At least in Weber's writings value-free social science did not imply 'presuppositionless' investigation of social reality (1949: 1-47) as it tends to be accepted in the present-day empirical sociology. Within the framework of accepted values and desired end-states it should still be possible for a social scientist to maintain the standards of objectivity, avoid distortion, and examine and present facts in a manner that is replicable, so that inter-subjective verifiability could be possible. Our position is that it is possible to distinguish between 'fact' and 'value' and to identify value-bias whenever it occurs in social inquiry. When we take this position we are aware of the tension inherent between the positivist and the intuitionist camps. This tension is apparent even in Weber's famous notion of 'understanding' or *verstehen* itself. It raises some far-reaching philosophical issues into which we need not go. According to Weber, 'action' covers all behaviour to which a subjective meaning is attached by the agents, and social action covers all action that takes account of the behaviour of others by virtue of the subjective meaning attached to it by the agents. Some interpreters of Weber have taken this sense of *verstehen* to entail an intuitionist position. But this is not so. Weber is emphatic that even the most self-evident interpretation requires to be validated by reference to concrete empirical evidence. In the choice of this evidence value-preferences may operate but verification of subjective meaning or interpretation, as in the case of all hypotheses, is indispensable. To that extent Weber never compromised with the basic tenets of positivism, although he always believed that some form of 'internal' comprehension and 'external' confirmation is necessary to justify any sociological explanation (Runciman, 1974: 11-13). Likewise, when we argue in favour of a value-based understanding of social reality, we believe that the test of empirical demonstration and verification (within the methodological canon of objectivity) is inescapable for committed social science inquiry.

In our view, suppression and distortion of basic facts are most injurious to one's own values, and they weaken the cause or the efforts in the direction of the desired end-states. Within the matrix of value-commitments, a certain objective methodology could be followed without any wavering on one's ultimate value-choices. For social scientists, therefore, the question of 'ends and means' is of vital importance. Neither is to be subordinated to the other. So far efforts were aimed at pursuing one at the expense of the other. Our submission is that it is possible to blend these two together. This will also end the 'ivory-tower' isolation of which social sciences are often held guilty, and will render them as socially relevant and serviceable. One of the reasons why the contribution of social scientists to social change in India is dismally poor is that they are pre-occupied with spinning theories 'of action' rather than 'for action'. Consequently, a philosophical theory of social reality seldom gets translated into an instrumentality of social transformation despite the rhetoric of demagogues and academicians who profess a deep concern for the wretched of the earth.

Notes

1. This is a revised version of a working paper prepared for a seminar on 'Interdisciplinary Approach to Social Reality—Its Methodology and Organization' held at the Tilak Maharashtra Vidyapeeth, Pune, in February 1981. It was also delivered as a lecture at the Department of Humanities and Social Sciences, Indian Institute of Technology, New Delhi, on 19 March 1981. Later it was published in *Philosophical Theory and Social Reality* (edited by Ravinder Kumar), Allied, 1984. These exposures have helped me a great deal in recasting the paper. I am particularly indebted to my colleague Dr. U.B. Bhoite who read the paper and made several comments.

2. These premises have been drawn from Berger and Luckmann, 1971: pp. 78-79.
3. It must be stressed that mathematics needs not be treated exclusively as a natural science. In their styles of reasoning as well as of abstraction mathematical and philosophical discourses have been quite akin to each other. This was as much true of the classical Greek philosophy as it is in the case of modern symbolic logic which draws heavily on Boolean Algebra. However, contemporary social sciences in general, and sociology in particular, gradually got dislocated from philosophical and also mathematical reasoning when methodological sophistication became euphemism for increased quantification and application of statistical techniques.
4. One could add to this list 'symbolic interactionism', 'ethnomethodology', 'phenomenology' and other perspectives too.
5. I must confess that before preparing this paper I had not carefully looked into Prof. Ramkrishna Mukherjee's *What Will It be*? (Bombay: Allied, 1976). I hope to go through this work carefully, and shall revise my views on his 'inductive sociology' in case I find that my apparently harsh judgement was unwarranted.
6. The term 'theory' has been used here to imply 'scientific explanation'—the sense in which it is commonly used in some of the standard works in the philosophy of science. For example see Nagle (1961) and Kaplan (1964).
7. I hope this should suffice to clarify that I am not arguing in favour of theoretical eclecticism or *laissez-faire.*
8. I have stated by position on this question elaborately elsewhere. See Dhanagare, 1980: pp. 25-26.

References

Althusser, L. and E. Balibạr, *Reading Capital* (Translated by Ben Brewster), New York: Pantheon Books, 1970, pp. 13-24.

Ball, Richard, A., 'The Dialectical Method: Its Application to Social Theory', *Social Forces*, 57 (3), March 1979, pp. 785-98.

Berger, Peter L. and T. Luckmann, *The Social Construction of Reality: A Treatise in the Sociology of Knowledge*, Harmondsworth: Penguin Books, 1971.

Bottomore, T.B. and M. Rubel (Eds.), *Karl Marx—Selected Writings in Sociology and Social Philosophy*, Penguin Books, 1971.

Damle, Y.B., 'For a Theory of Indian Sociology', in *Sociology in India* (Report of Seminar), 18-20 December 1964, Agra University, Institute of Social Sciences.

——, 'The School and College as a Social System', in M.S. Gore *et al.* (Eds.), *Papers in Sociology of Education in India*, New Delhi: NCERT, 1967, pp. 250-81.

Desai, A.R., *Social Background of Indian Nationalism*, Bombay: Oxford University Press, 1948.

——, 'Introduction to Rural Sociology in India', in A.R. Desai (ed.), Rural Sociology in India, Bombay: Popular Prakashan, 1969, pp. 1-99.

Dhanagare, D.N., 'Search for Identity' (Seminar Special Number on Studying our Society), No. 254 October, 1980, pp. 23-26.

Durkheim, E., *The Rules of Sociological Method* (8th edn. translated by S.A. Solovay & J.H. Mueller, and ed. by George E.G. Catlin), London: The Free Press, 1964.

Godelier, M., *Perspectives in Marxist Anthropology*, Cambridge University Press, 1976.

Gore, M.S., 'Inaugural Address', in Indian Institute of Advanced Study, Simla. *Social Sciences and Social Realities*, Simla, 1967, pp. 9-13.

Horton, J., 'Order and Conflict Theories of Social Problems as Competing Ideologies', *American Journal of Sociology*, Vol. 71, 1966, pp. 701-13.

Kaplan, A., *The Conduct of Inquiry: Methodology for Behavioural Science*, San Francisco: Chandler Pub. Co., 1964.

Knorr, K., 'Producing and Reproducing Knowledge: Descriptive or Constructive', *Social Science Information*, Vol. 16,1977, pp. 669-96.

Knorr-Cetina, K.D., 'Social and Scientific Method or What Do We Make of the Distinction Between the Natural and the Social Sciences?' *Philosophy of the Social Science*, Vol. 11, 1981, pp.335-59.

Kuhn, T., *The Structure of Scientific Revolution*, Chicago, 1970.

Mukherjee, R., *Trends in Indian Sociology* (reprinted from Current Sociology, Vol. 25, No.3), London: Sage Publications, 1977.

Mullick, M.I. (Ed.), *Social Enquiry: Goals and Approaches*, Delhi: Manohar, 1979.

Nagel, E., *Structure of Science: Problems in the Logic of Scientific Explanation*, New York: Harward Bruce & World Inc., 1961.

Parsons, T., *The Social System*, London: Routledge & Kegan Paul, 1970.

——, *The Structure of Social Action*, Delhi: Amerind Publishing (Indian edition), 1974.

Piaget, Jean, *Main Trends in Inter-Disciplinary Research* (Main Trends in the Social Sciences—Series 5), London: George Allen & Unwin Ltd., 1973.

Rex, John (Ed.), *Approaches to Sociology: An Introduction to Major Trends in British Sociology*, London: Routledge & Kegan Paul, 1974.

Runciman, W.G., *Social Science and Political Theory* (2nd edition), Cambridge University Press, 1974.

Singh, Y., *Modernization of Indian Tradition*, Delhi: Rawat Publications, 1983.

Srinivas, M.N., 'Sociology and Sociologists in India Today' (Presidential Address, Ninth All India Sociological Conference, Delhi), *Sociological Bulletin*, XIX (1), pp. 1-10, 1970.

Tournaine, A., *The Self-Production of Society* (Translated by D. Coltman), Chicago: University of Chicago Press, 1977.

Weber, Max, *The Methodology of the Social Sciences*, New York: The Free Press, 1949.

Chapter five

Kosambi, dialectical materialism and the structure and dynamics of Indian society

Social sciences in India today are virtually gripped by waves of indigenization. The disciplines of sociology and social anthropology are no exceptions to this trend. Search for alternative conceptual tools and theoretical approaches seems to have developed a kind of xenophobia towards the so-called imported concepts and theories. "So-called"—because 'materialist thinking or interpretation' has not been alien to the indigenous philosophical tradition in India. However, dialectical materialism and class-analysis, which are now attributed to the Marxist intellectual tradition, evoked considerable resistance in the Indian intelligentsia in general and social scientists in particular. The resistance could also be due to the earlier link up between Marxism and Communism, when if one was a Marxist one was also generally a member of the Communist Party of India. Thus, 'intellectual Marxism' was practically unknown. The initial neglect of D.D. Kosambi's brilliant works cannot be explained otherwise.

That there is a renewed interest in Kosambi's studies in Indian history is evident in the institution of a memorial lecture series in his name at the Bombay University and an occasional lecture series in Poona as well as in the publication of collections of his writings (e.g., DDKHS, SSP). Though this late recognition is visible in the professional circles of historians in India, other social scientists, particularly Indian sociologists and social anthropologists have seldom turned their attention to Kosambi's insightful sociological analysis of ancient Indian society, culture and civilization. Partly this was due to sociologists lack of familiarity with the enormous historical evidence that Kosambi marshalled from his investigations of the proto-historic and ancient period, and partly due to their late realization of the relevance of history itself for a sound sociological understanding of Indian society.

As it is now a commonplace argument, any revolution in scientific thinking and knowledge comes about not through the accumulation of data alone but primarily through a change in the paradigm.[1] What matters is the type of questions an analyst raises or hypotheses one formulates. Kosambi's achievements lie precisely in his path-breaking formulations that brought a major shift in the paradigms that were in vogue in Indian history (Thapar, 1980: 565-66). The purpose of this paper is to put together Kosambi's ideas on science and history, his understanding of dialectical materialism and his rigorous attempts to apply it to the understanding of Indian society—its structure and dynamics through history. Quintessentially this exercise is more compilative rather than evaluative in nature. It has been attempted with a view to draw attention to serious applications of the Marxian paradigm by a non-practising historian and sociologist whose writings can provide important directions to cognitive structures of Indian sociology and social anthropology. First part of this paper deals with Kosambi's views on science and history as well as his exposition of 'dialectical materialism' as he understood it. His analysis of the Indian society—its structure and the stages of its historical development—has been summarized in the second part. Part third concludes with Kosambi's major contribution to social analysis.

I

Kosambi viewed science and society as closely interrelated. To him this dictum was true as much of social history as of Marxism as a science. Great scientific discoverers and discoveries cannot be separated from their social context social environment. For the understanding of social history, Kosambi stressed the most fundamental relationship between great discoverers and their social environment. Conservatives take history as the personal achievement of great men, specifically the history of science. 'The Marxist tradition, however, asserts that the great man is he who finds some way to fulfil a deep perhaps unstated social need of his time' (DDKHS: ix). Therefore, Kosambi argued that 'no Marxist would claim science to be independent of the social system, within which the scientist must function' (SSP: 12). He thus takes a definite and an unequivocal materialist position in the sociology of knowledge.

If Marxism is to be treated as a science in its own right, then it must be recognized that its distinctive method of analysis is the method of dialectical materialism. Like G. Lukacs (1971: 2-24), even Kosambi thought that 'dialectical materialism contained the essence of Marxism'. It is a complete science—an analytical system and set of principles for organizing knowledge—which is known after the genius who first developed its theory and used it systematically as a tool of social inquiry (EE: 1). In elucidating the basics of dialectical materialism, Kosambi followed the standard texts. According to him, dialectical materialism holds that matter is the most primeval and substantive reality whose properties are inexhaustible, whereas mind is simply an aspect of matter, being a function of the brain. Following Marx's logic in turning the Hegelian idealism upside down, Kosambi also asserted that 'far from being primary phenomena, ideas are mere reflection of material processes and changes upon human consciousness which is itself a material process' (EE: 1).

Materialism thus constitutes a complete philosophy and the most coherent theory of history. The basic concepts that form integral parts of this Marxist framework, are elucidated by Kosambi with relative ease and characteristic clarity. 'Matter itself is not inert', he said 'but in a constant state of interaction and change; it is a complex of processes and unfolds its inexhaustible properties in its interaction with environment'. In every stage, Kosambi stresses, there resides an inherent quality of change, an 'inner contradiction' which leads eventually to a negation of that stage or condition. Highlighting the dialectics as a law of development, he further points out that the negation is quite naturally again negated. There is thus a fundamental unity of opposites. 'Life is a mode of existence of certain forms of matter. Its characteristic mode of existence is that, in order to preserve its special quality as living matter, it has to interact with a suitable environment. In the context of human life and society, this environment is furnished to a large extent by the society itself (EE: 1-2).

Since man cannot exist without bread 'an aggregate of human beings becomes a society when and only when the people develop the most essential relations, i.e., relations developed through production and mutual exchange of commodities'. Kinship is not as essential a relation as are production relations. The rate and the quantity of interaction of men with natural surroundings depend on the techniques of production. This implies that the surplus production depends upon the means of production. The method by which the surplus passes into the hands of the ultimate user is determined by and in turn determines the form of society, the relations of production (CCAI: 10-11). It means that the distribution of the surplus (product) among the various members of society is a matter for the relations of production (EE: 2). What matters is 'who owns the tools, the land, who controls the disposal of the surplus, and who regulates quality and form of supply'. Therefore, society is held together by bonds of production' (Preface, AISIH: xii-xiii). Hence, far from depicting materialism as a source of destruction of human values, as its critics often did, Kosambi thought that it actually showed how human values—whether divine, moral or legal—are related to contemporary conditions of social existence. This formulation of Kosambi was clearly a cogent restatement of some of the key propositions from Marx's famous preface to *A Contribution to the Critique of Political Economy* (c.f. Marx, 1977b: 19-23).

It is these materialist premises that underlie Kosambi's conception of history also. To him history was not simply narrative chronology of episodes, dynasties and kings or tales of war and battle. History is a reconstructed profile of society—a chart of societal development could ever be fully understood by mere study of philosophical systems—however great or lofty these might be (MR: 1). He, therefore, defined history 'as the presentation, in chronological order of successive developments in the means and relations of production (AISIH: I; CCAI: 10). The production relations could be found at the root of several Indian myths and ritual practices only if the analyst cared to trace them. However, although Kosambi had decried the neglect of such materialist analysis, he also warned historians against 'crass materialism' which can be no substitute for a systematic understanding of Indian culture and society (MR: 2).

Since all historical reconstructions have to depend on intrinsic source-material, what truly matters is the quality of sources. In general, available source-material is inadequate, at times even poor in India. Any exclusive reliance on either epigraphic finds, archaeological excavation work, or on numismatic data, or philological and euphemistic reconstructions, according to Kosambi, would not take us very far if each of these is used to the exclusion of others. The best course open while attempting historical reconstruction is to combine all of these sources whenever they are found to be these may have to be further reinforced by ethnographic and anthropological field studies too (SSP: 10). But the focus unquestionably has to be on 'identifying successive developments in the means and relations of production'. It is these which truly mirror the life of people lived at any period (AISIH: 3-6). Kosambi had thus made his choice in favour of a 'purely materialistic reconstruction of history and of stages of societal development'. The choice is justified on the grounds that man has all along been making himself by using tools (of production) in order to live increasingly well at the cost of his environment. And with every new basic discovery in the means of production follow important social consequences like sudden rise in the human population etc. Moreover, 'no social organization can be more advanced than the instruments of production will allow' at that point of time (AISIH: 6-7). Even this position of Kosambi is in conformity with the classical Marxian proposition that 'stages of societal development necessarily correspond to the stages of development of mode of production (Marx, 1977b: 19-23). The long quotation from Karl Marx's preface to his *Critique of Political Economy* cited by

Kosambi (AISIH: 9) confirms that this approach to the study of Indian society culture and civilization, through comparative historical reconstruction, implied a clear-cut and definite theory of history known as dialectical materialism, also called Marxism' (AISIH: 8).

What pace do studies on religion, superstitions, rituals and myths have in the study of the material foundations of any societal development? In this regard, Kosambi has warned us against excessive concentration on the study of such superstructural categories as it would inevitably lead us away from history. But this is not to suggest that superstructure ought to be neglected. Ideas are important but not in themselves; they are important as products of certain types of social structure and hence can be used as source-material for deducing both information and insights about social structure. Sometimes, material changes in the forces of production may have to be reconstructed, or even extrapolated from 'what survives as marks upon the ideological superstructure'. Ideas too develop into a force once they have gripped the masses; these supply the form in which men become conscious of their conflicts and fight them out (cf. Marx, 1977a: 133-57 and *Manifesto*: 57-63). Studies in superstructure sometimes do reveal the real changes occurring in the base. Thus, studying tribal cults or tracing a local God through village tradition can give a priceless clue to ancient migrations, primitive tracks and trade-routes and the merger of cattle-breeding tribesmen with food-gatherers which led to firm agricultural settlement (SSP: 11)[2]. What is most striking is that even after adhering to the basic Marxist methodology of analyzing the base-superstructure relationship, Kosambi affirms his conviction that 'Marxism is not a plain and simple economic determinism as its opponents often take it to be'. Instead he projected it more as an 'intelligent determinism that discusses conditions rather than causes and one that takes full cognizance of the course of historical development' (AISIH: 9-10).

On the question as to whether Marxism is a deterministic system of analysis Kosambi has clarified his position thus:

> Our position has also to be very far from a mechanical determinism particularly in dealing with India, where form

> is given the utmost importance while content is ignored. Economic determinism will not do. It is not inevitable, nor even true, that a given amount of wealth will lead to a given type of development. (Hence) the complete historical process through which the social form has been reached is also of prime importance.

This position of Kosambi is only a restatement of the clarification which F. Engels offered in his letter to J. Bloch, suggesting that the materialist conception of history implied 'production and reproduction of real-life as the ultimately determining element in history' and that more than this neither Marx nor he had ever asserted (Marx and Engels, 1958: ii 488). Therefore, Dale Riepe (1974: 42) preferred to describe Kosambi as a 'cultural determinist' rather than an 'economic determinist'[3]. Kosambi only believed that economic considerations are enormously important even in the explanation of religions. 'Being a histomat Kosambi tended to emphasize productive base as a source of explanation rather than putting emphasis on the superstructure' (Riepe, 1974: 42).

All that Marx wrote was not taken by Kosambi as sacrosanct. Adoption of Marx's thesis does not mean blind repetition of all his conclusions. Sounding like a true non-conformist, Kosambi particularly cautions a scrupulous student of Marxism as a scientific methodology and theory of history not to confuse it with those of the official party-line Marxists. Similarly, Kosambi always emphasized the distinction between Marx's interpretation of western society and that of Asian society. Whereas his substantive concern was with the former, he only used the Asian setting for occasional illustrative purposes. At any rate the general theory of history founded on dialectical materialism is independent of the two concrete settings. Writings on these may reveal certain misjudgements or lacunae which ought to be understood in terms of social conditions in which certain interpretations were offered whether on European or on Asian society. Therefore, without an iota of hesitation a Marxist Kosambi dismisses some of Marx's writings on India, particularly the formulations in the context of the Asiatic mode of production, as 'misleading' (AISIH: 10-11). For constructing a Marxist theory of Indian society, Kosambi thought that Marx's writings on the Asiatic mode were not particularly relevant or germane[4].

No science and scientific theory provides the last word in the quest for knowledge. Marxism as a scientific theory must not be an exception to this basic premise in the philosophy of science. To Kosambi what was needed was a sensible extension of Marxian theory by taking stock of later studies under Marx's direct inspiration. Here Kosambi has cited Engels' famous study of the nature and decay of tribal organization, of property relations and the way he demonstrated how forms of family, marriage and the state corresponded to types of property (Engels, 1957). Only more rigorous and systematic applications help us to weed out some of the redundant conclusions of Marx and would ensure further enrichment of Marxism as a scientific theory (AISIH: 13). In this matter party hardliners often tend to take Marxism as an inelastic, inflexible and irrefutable law of social development. This attitude practically turned 'a science' into 'the dogma' which Kosambi always found irreconcilable with his positivist and scientific convictions. He was also conscious of the fact that the conclusions of his studies on ancient Indian culture and society, based on a rigorous application of the 'mode of production' framework, would have a mixed reception because of his repeated references to Marx because 'official Marxists always looked with suspicion upon the work of an outsider' (SSP: 11).

About his intellectual commitment to Marxism, Kosambi made no secret. On the contrary he proudly proclaimed it. In his letter to Daniel Ingalls, Kosambi has presented his classification of the intelligentsia vis-a-vis Marxism. Kosambi has divided the world into three groups: those (i) swearing by Marxism, (ii) swearing at Marxism, and (iii) indifferent, i.e., just swearing, but forced by the crisis to shift to either (i) or (ii). Without mincing words or searching for convenient covers to camouflage his true identity as a scholar, Kosambi placed himself in the first category (Ingalls, 1974: 29). But far from treating Marxism as a craft for political propaganda, he stressed more on using it sensibly as a scientific methodol ogy.

> The point...is not to prove Marxism or to support it, but to use a certain well-proved line of approach to draw conclusions from (such) meagre evidence as exists (Ingalls, 1974: 29).

This explains why Kosambi was intolerant towards any form of hypocrisy, inefficiency and dogmatism (Basham, 1974: 18). The dogmatists, both at home and abroad, were not spared by him. He unsparingly castigated the orientalists in Moscow as 'pseudo-Marxist scholars' and the 'non-sense' they produced at the Institute of Oriental Studies. He poured this scathing criticism on Moscow orientalists when Kosambi was in fact a guest of the U.S.S.R. Academy of Sciences. Only a scholar with the courage of his conviction, as Kosambi was, could offer such an 'unusual gift' to his academic hosts. The Soviet scholars, of course, did not fail to return the 'compliment'; they thought 'Kosambi's Marxism' was only 'skin-deep' (Ingalls, 1974: 31-32). At times even his best friends thought that Kosambi's historical interpretations, particularly those based on statistical analyses of the punch-marked coins, though most convincing, sometimes contained errors and misinterpretations, because he often appeared to be attempting to force his data into a rather doctrinaire pattern (Basham, 1984: 18). It is indeed beyond our competence to comment on, let alone assess or ascertain, the degree of doctrinaire assertions in Kosambi's historical interpretations on the ancient Indian culture and civilization which he always based on systematic and rigorous use of archaeological and numismatic data. However, if he were really dogmatic or a doctrinaire Marxist, whom something other than a genuine desire to search for truth had motivated to look back on history, he would have exercised a calculated moderation in his criticism of Moscow orientalists, or of 'official Marxists' at home.

Kosambi's critique of Dange's (1961) book *India from Primitive Communism to Slavery* was no less pungent. He thought that such a work by one of the founders of the Communist Party of India was 'painfully disappointing' being full of errors of fact and of reasoning and hence replete with 'endless confusion' (DDKHS:

7b). Kosambi attributed these errors to Dange's uncritical acceptance of the Sanskrit documents as the best sources for historical investigation. Kosambi refuted Dange's view that 'the concept of *yuga* exemplified the Hindu system of looking at history and that it considered history as being not static but always moving and changing'. To Kosambi this supposedly dynamic Hindu treatment of history was the obliteration of all historical content (DDKHS: 74). Kosambi found Dange's characterization of 'Brahman as the Aryan commune and *yajnya* as its means of production as particularly repugnant.' Pointing out that Rigvedic uses of Brahman could be, and in fact should be, explained as referring to prayer or to priesthood while *yajnya* was the fire sacrifice, Kosambi asserted that a ritual cannot be a mode of production though ancient man must have understood magic and ritual as helping to increase production. Hence, Dange's interpretation of Brahman and *yajnya* as primitive Aryan commune with the collective mode of production was dismissed by Kosambi as 'ridiculous' (DDKHS: 74-75). Equally unpalatable and unacceptable to him was Dange's view that the *varna* system was a later development representing a division of labour and that Dasyus, frequently referred to, in Vedic literature, were pure chattel-slaves. On the contrary Kosambi stressed the fact of some form of coercive mechanism—the state was always visible in the Vedas which implied some form of class division as well, whether fully crystallized or not. Therefore, the formation of the Shudra as a social category, into which a large portion of the Dasyus were thrust, actually prevented the development of real slavery in India. Kosambi then suggests that because of the caste-*varna* system India had helotage, not slavery (DDKHS: 76-77; AISIH: 196-97). Forms of slavery actually increased in India only after 'feudalism from above' was introduced. We shall return to this point later.

II

This brings us to the basic structure of Indian society and the stages of its development through history as Kosambi viewed them. The most important clues to the understanding of this development in the Indian past was the basic factor of transition from a tribal structure—a pre-class social formation—to caste structure. According to Kosambi, what primarily accounted for this transition was the introduction of plough agriculture which changed the system of production. It could now produce surplus which, in settled village communities, became profit for the priestly class. This is how, he argues, the changed system of production broke the structure of tribal and clan organization and made caste an alternative social organization (AISIH: 24-25; CCAI: 170-71). Tribal clans and totems changed into caste names. Since Brahmanical settlements were the chief agency through which basic changes in agricultural production were setting in, this process of transformation inevitably led to eventual absorption and assimilation of tribal local cults into the Brahmanical tradition and in Sanskritization of folk cults. 'With virtual monopoly over land and ritual, Brahminism could peacefully reduce tribes to castes' (AISIH: 317-20). Kosambi has cited numerous examples—one of which pertains to peasant surnames in Maharashtra which show that clantotemic *devaks* survived after the tribal groups had dissolved and merged into castes and sub-castes (AISIH: 33)[5].

The caste system since then persisted as, and even now continues to be, the most important aspect of Indian social structure. It is a ubiquitous and powerful institution, particularly in Hindu society although some non-Hindus including Muslims and Christians could not escape its overpowering impact. However, what is most striking is that it has survived the onslaught of Buddhism in the distant past and of Christianity in the more recent one. Kosambi cites examples of 'good Roman Catholics in Goa who regard themselves as Brahmin Christians and prefer to take drinking water or food from a Hindu Brahmin but not from a Shudra Christian' (Kosambi, 1944: 243). Of course, conversion from a caste-based society would in part account for this phenomenon. But the great diversity of features of the caste system, at the level of both its precepts and practices, is such that any statement of a general nature about Indian castes, according to Kosambi, can be contradicted, whether it is about customs of food, marriage, or about hierarchical ranking based on purity-pollution dimension[6], or even about internal divisions into sub-castes or on occupational differences and specialization (DDKHS: 127-8).

The sources of these contradictions within the caste system are not far to seek. Kosambi argues that 'the caste system was designed to preserve Indian society in a static mould. Its principal function now is the negation of history and therewith the negation of progress' (Kosambi, 1944: 245-46). Though in theory the system was rigid and inflexible, its practice varied from region to region depending upon the stage of development of productive forces. For example, the caste system was never strong enough in Kashmir where a developed form of feudalism emerged. Here Kosambi observes the notorious laxity of observances on the part of Kashmiri Brahmins. Apart from this slackness, the class behaviour of the Brahmins forfeited their sanctity to a considerable extent as most of them were landholders or government officials and had fought on the battlefield, with arms in hand, purely for personal material advancement unconnected with any religious, ritual or theological considerations. The Kashmiri Brahmins had thus acted in history more as a class of holders of land-grants (*agrahara*), as feudal barons fighting against the suzerainty of the central power of the king, paving way for the ultimate victory of feudalism (DDKHS: 115-18). The growth of commerce and trade particularly that of the precious saffron further accelerated the process of weakening of central power and the rise of feudalism. Consequently, the caste system in Kashmir was, in contrast to the rest of India, too thin a disguise for that of classes. The *agrahara* became a hereditary *jagir* form of private property in land (DDKHS: 118).

In Kosambi's assessment, the main features of contemporary Hinduism developed only after the Mohammedan penetration of India. Hence, the Hinduism as we have today is not entirely the same as the religion of the Vedic Aryans. Modern Hinduism, along with its caste system, has not only survived the inroads of Islam and Christianity but was entirely transformed by Buddhism that prevailed in India for centuries (Kosambi, 1944:245-46). The Buddhist philosophy of non-violence, originally borrowed from a much older religion—Jainism—has now become an integral part of Hinduism. The rapid spread of Buddhism, first in India and subsequently beyond the Indian frontier to China, Japan, Asia Minor, Tibet and Mongolia has to be understood, according to Kosambi, in terms of the development of productive relations, trade and the historical tendencies of that period. To him, 'caste in the Buddhist period was quite close to the class system' (Kosambi, 1944: 245), but its stronghold was nearer the Indus-valley region than Magadh as it was more rigid and conservative a system in the former than in the latter. However, despite its contempt for Brahminism and for the sacrificial rituals at which Brahmins presided as priests, Kosambi argues:

> Buddhism did not touch the older ritual, nor set up a new one of its own; it worked out a new social scheme without touching caste which would make people more civilized, make it possible for them to co-exist with less friction (DDKHS: 130).

The Hinduism could stage a comeback partly because the salient features of Buddhism including the economically dispensable vegetarianism had been absorbed by Brahminism. The capacity for synthesis and assimilation in the caste Hindu society was so profound as to admit Buddha as an incarnation of Vishnu (Kosambi, 1944: 247-48). It is this adaptability of the *varna*-caste system that enabled other regions to be opened up. Its flexibility, its post-Buddhist development into a method for maintaining the status of any rule that made nominal concessions to Hinduism, enabled the caste system to survive great changes. Though paradoxical, the progressive function of caste in a sense ended with the establishment of the basic agricultural economy, based on the foundation of the village unit and family as a sub-unit. Thereafter, caste mainly became a stabilizing force itself attempting to become static.

Kosambi attempted to identify the content and features of development of Indian society through various stages of history. But in doing so he was averse to applying mechanically and uncritically the accepted Marxist periodisation of European history to the Indian past (Thapar, 1980: 377). On slavery, which is the first stage of historical development of modes of production, as the Marxist general theory of history has suggested, Kosambi firmly argued that Indian slavery was not strictly speaking a variant of that ubiquitous, though ignoble, institution in the ancient period. Indian slavery was not even recognizable by the Greek and Roman standards. Chattel slavery could never have had any significant role in production process in India. Though in the classical European economy human beings were traded like cattle for heavy labour in mines and fields, this was never so in India. *Dasa* and Shudra were synonymous. This class of labour was also expropriated by the Aryans but eventually absorbed into the Aryan-fold as a class of servants, bondsmen as helots but not slaves (DDKHS: 82-83).

The feudal mode of production is the only stage of historical development, as periodised by Marxists, which Kosambi accepted as relevant in the Indian context. Even in this regard he did not apply the European model of feudalism blindly; rather he introduced the distinction between 'feudalism from above' and 'feudalism from below'. Kosambi thought these were peculiar features of Indian feudalism. 'Feudalism from above' referred to a state wherein a central authority, be it an emperor or a powerful king, levied tributes from subordinate chieftains who were still effective rulers in their own respective territories and who were left undisturbed so long as they paid the supreme central authority. 'These subordinate rulers managed the land administration in their jurisdiction directly without a class of revenue/tax collecting intermediaries' (AISIH: 295-96). This is the kind of feudal formation that, according to Kosambi, developed through changes which came about in the late first millennium A.D. subsequent to the Gupta period (Thapar, 1980: 378-79). Indian feudalism, therefore, differed substantively from its European counterpart—which he characterized as 'feudalism from below'. It implied a class of landowners developed within settled village communities, between the state and the peasantry, gradually wielding armed power over the local population. It is this class which is the *de facto* ruler in the local communities and which claimed a direct relationship with the state. The relationship was reciprocal—the state conceding (rather helplessly) the right of tax collection by small intermediaries who passed on a fraction to the feudal hierarchy in contrast to the direct collection by royal officials in 'feudalism from above' (AISIH: 295-96). In return the feudal lords furnished military assistance to the state whenever required.

The similarity between the European and Indian variants of feudalism was found in that in both the cases techniques of production were simple, being at a low level of development: production—largely individual in character—was for the immediate subsistence needs of a household or a village community. Also there was increasing commodity production. But, 'demense-farming on the lord's estate by compulsory labour service'—a key feature of European feudalism—was decidedly not true of India. Political centralization was common to both India and Europe and so was conditional holding of land by lords on some kind of service-tenures (particularly noticeable among Rajput chiefs and among the earlier Muslims, whose chiefs were invaders). But, all lords were required to serve and their *jagirs* shifted from time to time. Parasitism of courtiers, whose offices were seldom hereditary, practically bordered on a new form of slavery (DDKHS: 93-94). A more striking difference lies in the fact that patrimonial justice, which formed a part of the lord's functions in the European model, was either absent or developed only in parts of India where village councils could be displaced by lords possessing armed forces of their own (AISIH: 353-55).

Kosambi pointed out three more notable features distinguishing Indian from European feudalism—the increase of slavery, absence of guilds, and the lack of an organized church (AISIH: 355). However, growth of castes, and the rapid transformation of tribal into caste structures obviated the need for both guild and church. But with the expansion of caste and settled self-sufficient agricultural communities the commodity production went down per head of population. Hence, feudalism from above became necessary for increasing commodity production to match the steadily growing trade. The traders themselves could not have fulfilled this need except when they turned 'barons'—a term that has specific meaning in European history. Hence, private landowners and/or the feudal barons became necessary in India (DDKHS: 101). This explains further why 'slavery became more prominent than before in Indian feudalism. Without being indispensable to the means of production the slaves formed the nucleus of the manpower that the barons needed to make them independent of the peasantry. They were used not only as specifically privileged armed retainers, but also as commodity producers—particularly of cloth and other specialized goods—at least a part of which was traded either directly by landlords or barons themselves or through dependent trading class. To supplement the paid labour feudal landlords often preferred to cultivate special plots of land for themselves and their families, but with deployment of this slave (bonded) labour instead of leasing out the land to peasant tenants' (DDKHS: 102). In Kosambi's view all these features of Indian feudalism appeared on the scene during the fourteenth century in the reign of Firuz Tughlaq[7] (DDKHS: 102).

Indian feudalism did not fail to produce its own ideology. In his papers on the *Bhagvad Gita*, Kosambi has attempted to show how this sacred document propounded the concept of *bhakti*—laying emphasis on unquestioning faith in and personal loyalty and devotion to a deity. These values were in conformity with the ideology of feudalism. It did not challenge any preceding doctrines except Vedic *yajna* (CCAI: 206-07) but *Gita* could not promote any fundamental change in the means of production either. Instead 'it furnished one scriptural source in which anything could be read without denying the validity of a class system, and without violence to accepted Brahmin methodology' (DDKHS: 165-69). Kosambi has argued that the essence of fully developed feudalism is the chain of personal loyalty which binds retainer to chief, tenant to lord and baron to king or emperor. Such a social structure had developed in India only during or after the sixth century and to hold this type of society and its state together the best religion is one which preached devotion and loyalty. *Gita* was thus a logical performance for the early Gupta period in which its message of *bhakti* and personal faith served the purpose of sustaining feudal society (CCAI: 208). The text emphasized caste functions and preached an ethic which required people to perform their ordained duties even during periods of frequent and deepening crisis (DDKHS: 180-81) to ensure increased commodity production that had begun to decline with the rise of caste system and self-reliant village communities. It was the ideological basis of Indian feudal society (CCAI: 208). Therefore, although the later *bhakti*—devotional—tradition, from Samkara (C.A.D. 800) through Dhyaneshwar, Tukaram and other saint poets down to Tilak and Gandhi, became a powerful instrument of mobilizing various social groups (Thapar, 1980: 368) it could not truly transform the social consciousness of the lower classes (AISIH: 127-28).

The third major stage of development, namely, the bourgeois epoch in Indian history, according to Kosambi, coincided with the British rule. In studying this modern phase he applied the conceptual categories of class-analysis again drawn from Marxism. The growth of the class of indigenous bourgeoisie was facilitated by pre-existing compredor elements. Kosambi has mentioned people from Gujarat, Kathiawad and Kutch, who were not necessarily traders, but are occupying a prominent place in the capitalist class in post-independence India. This was possible largely because their early contacts with Mohammedan traders and rulers enabled this small fraction to develop early contacts with British, and thereby introduced them to the new system of production, i.e., production based on machinery and modern capital (EE: 12-13). Parsis are the best example of how a minority community could become the most advanced, cultured and powerful, first as compredors and later adopting modern industrial and financial capital. Marwaris for a long time confined themselves to financing and money-lending though lately they too turned towards industrial manufacturing. What sıruck Kosambi most is the remarkable unity of class interests of the Indian bourgeoisie (CCAI: 2-3). In contrast there has been a progressive deterioration in the living conditions of peasantry, factory workers, low-paid office workers and intellectuals. It was the Indian bourgeoisie which was primarily interested in building a strong nationalist movement to counter the growing hegemony of the British bourgeoisie. This was possible only by establishing an axis with peasant masses in the countryside and working class in cities. The Congress under Gandhi and Nehru, to Kosambi, had basically served as a bridge between the Indian bourgeoisie and the masses. With the transfer of power it is the Indian capitalist class which has monopolised power (CCAI: 3-6). Kosambi is therefore highly critical of Gandhian leadership of the mass movements of the 1920s and 1930s as well as of Nehru's development planning in the first decade and half after independence (EE: 6-9, 10-18).

A gradual decline of feudalism was the corollary of the rise of bourgeois capitalism in India under the British rule. In 1857 Indian feudalism did try its strength against the British bourgeoisie but unsuccessfully. The post-Mutiny years saw the same feudal elements and *rajas* seeking British protection, privilege and patronage. Some of them, of course, moved into entrepreneurial industrial ventures and joined the ranks of the bourgeoisie. Even those who were liquidated after independence through a series of progressive legislation received fabulous compensations. In short, although formally Indian feudalism declined, 'the old ruling class was partially amalgamated into the new'. The two World Wars had accelerated this process which was only completed after the independence (DDKHS: 133-36).

In general, Kosambi's treatment of the bourgeois epoch of Indian history has streaks of populist assertions. Unlike his analysis of the earlier stages of development of Indian society and social structure in which his analytical insights are not only matched but even excelled by the meticulously collected evidence from archaeological, numismatic and ethnographic investigations, his study appears to have been fashioned primarily on the famous work of R. Palme Dutt's *India Today*[8]. Although Kosambi's observations on the capitalist stage of societal development in India are substantially correct, as several later studies have proved them to be, his style of argument while dealing with the bourgeois, capitalist phase departs considerably from the canons of scientific rigour that he had adhered to in his works on ancient and early medieval periods of Indian history.

III

This shortcoming, however, must not detract us from Kosambi's otherwise brilliant attempts to use 'dialectical materialism and class analysis', i.e., the Marxist paradigm in systematically understanding the structure and dynamics of Indian society. It needs, however, to be stressed that Kosambi's originality lies not only in his bringing about a major shift in paradigm, from chronological narrative to comparative analytical history, or in his cogent demonstration of how stages of societal change and development correspond to the successive stages in the development of means and relations of production as all Marxist analysts do, but mainly in his three contributions, or in the points he emphatically made. First, that positivist empiricist spirit is inescapable for building a sound understanding of complex social phenomena. Ideas/interpretations and facts considered in isolation from each other are of questionable validity. Hence, even Indology—more specifically that branch dealing with interpretation of ancient texts—and linguistic studies of problems of ancient Indian culture would be more fruitful if supplemented by archaeological, sociological, anthropological, numismatic and ethnographic evidence and vice-versa. Available data in each of these fields ought to be augmented by a great deal of honest and competent field work. None of the various techniques can, by itself, lead to any valid conclusion about ancient India; combined empirical operations are indispensable[9]. Secondly, Marxian dialectical materialism as a general theory and philosophy of history is unquestionably a useful paradigm with profound explanatory potential regardless of stages of societal development one addresses oneself to. However, the Marxian paradigm must not be mechanically applied to the understanding of Indian social reality. Facts will be the ultimate arbiter, and this dictum is doubly true in understanding a socio-culturally plural as well as complex Indian society. Studies of superstructure are therefore equally relevant and useful provided they adopt the dialectical materialist model sensibly. Hence, finally, neither Indian scriptures nor Marxism is sacrosanct; an analyst must continually separate myth from reality and endlessly discover innovative potentialities that the practice of synthesizing the two offers in understanding the structure and dynamics of Indian society.

In addition to these it must also be stressed that for Kosambi the dialectical understanding of the historical development of Indian society is not just a plain and simple exercise in the 'so-called' value-neutral science. To him, the specific feature of Indian history, viz., progressive exploitation of the worker under a dual burden of caste and class, cannot long remain buried under such vainglorious praise of Indian 'culture and philosophy'; it will not prevent the internal struggle for maturing all the more rapidly (DDKHS: 71). Being a Marxist by conviction, a robust optimism pervades Kosambi's views on future transformation of Indian society. He accepted Marxism not just as a scientific discipline that aids only in the interpretation of the past, but also as a living discipline which must continually work successfully with newer discoveries to serve as a guide to future action (EE: 2-3). Therefore, in stressing that 'it is doubtless more important to change history than to write it' (CCAI: Preface, xi), Kosambi was only emphatically reiterating the famous Marxist dictum. He certainly implied that historiography as an intellectual craft—itself a social product—ought to promote that internal struggle and contribute to the development of transformative forces from within.

These points deserve the serious attention of Indian sociologists and social anthropologists. By acquainting themselves with the Marxian paradigm as used with rigour by Kosambi, they have much to gain both in substantive, theoretical and in methodological terms.

Abbreviations Used for Kosambi's Works

AISIH – An Introduction to the Study of Indian History
CCAI – The Culture and Civilization of Ancient India in Historical Outline

DDKHS – D.D. Kosambi on History and Society (a volume edited by A.J. Syed)
EE – Exasperating Essays
MR – Myth and Reality
SSP – Science, Society and Peace (a collection brought out by the Academy of Political and Social Studies, Pune)

Notes

1. This position is taken on the basis of T. Kuhn (1970).
2. Kosambi has demonstrated this ably in his study of "Mother—Cult-Sites". See MR: 82-109.
3. Riepe's formulation 'cultural determinism' is in a sense begging the question, for, how does one define 'culture'? In Kosambi's view, conceptualiaztion of culture was inseparable from the productive forces and processes of their development.
4. For details of Marx's writings on India, see S. Avineri (1969).
5. More examples of these are available in Chapter-II in AISIH. Also see R. Thapar (1980: 371-2).
6. This aspect of caste system in India has been specifically highlighted by Louis Dumont (1972).
7. The basic question is: Did this feature of what Kosambi saw as 'Indian' variety of feudalism apply to all parts of the country or even to the predominant areas? Of late this question has been debated among historians. Its scope and magnitude prevent us from examining it in detail within the ambit of this paper.
8. We are offering this more as a studied guess. Because nowhere in his works Kosambi ever cited R. Palme Dutt's writings, which may also be because of his aversion for "OMs" (Official Marxists). But the tenor of Kosambi's characterization of the Indian bourgeoisie and its linkages with the Indian National Congress, has a striking resemblance with Palme Dutt's. For details see R. Palme Dutt (1947).
9. See D.D. Kosambi (1974: 1-27).

References

Avineri, S. (Ed.) 1969 *Karl Marx on Colonialism and Modernization*, New York: Anchor Books.

Basham, A.L. 1974 'Baba—A Personal Tribute', in Sharma (Ed.), *Indian Society*.

Dange, S.A. 1961 *India from Primitive Communism to Slavery* (4th Edition), New Delhi: People's Publishing House.

Dumont, I. 1972 *Homo Hierarchicus—The Caste System and Its Implications*, London: Paladin.

Dutt, Rajni P. 1947 *India Today*, Bombay: People's Publishing House.

Engels, P. 1957 *The Origin of the Family, Private Property and the State*, Moscow: Foreign Languages Publishing House.

Ingalls, Daniel H. H. 1974 'My Friendship with D.D. Kosambi', in Sharma (Ed.), *Indian Society*.

Kosambi, D.D. 1944 'Caste and Class in India', *Science and Society*, Vol. VIII, pp. 243-49.

Kosambi, D.D. 1956 *An Introduction to the Study of Indian History*, Bombay: Popular Prakashan.

1957 *Exasperating Essays* (Exercises in the Dialectical Method). Poona: People's Book House.

1962 *Myth and Reality-Studies in the Formation of Indian Culture*, Bombay: Popular Prakashan.

1965 *The Culture and Civilisation of Ancient India in Historical Outline*, London: Routledge and Kegan Paul.

1974 'Combined Methods in Indology', in *Science and Human Progress* (Prof. D.D. Kosambi Commemoration Volume), Bombay: Popular Prakashan, pp. 1-27.

1986 *Science Society and Peace* (Collection of Essays Compiled by the Academy of Political and Studies, Pune), Pune: Sudhir Bedekar (on behalf of the Academy).

Kuhn, T. 1970 *The Structure of Scientific Revolution*, Chicago: University Press.

Lukacs, Georg 1971 *History and Class Consciousness—Studies in Marxist Dialectics*, London: Merlin Press.

Marx, K. 1977a *Economic and Philosophic Manuscripts of 1844*, Moscow: Progress Publishers.

—— 1977b *A Contribution to the Critique of Political Economy*, Moscow: Progress Publishers.

Marx, K. and Engels, F. 1958 *Selected Works*, Moscow: Foreign Language Publishing House.

——*Manifesto of the Communist Party*, Moscow: Progress Publishers.

Riepe, D. 1974 'D.D. Kosambi: Father of Scientific Indian History', in R.S. Sharma (Ed.), *Indian Society*, pp. 34-44.

Sharma, R.S. (Ed.) 1974 *Indian Society: Historical Probings in Memory of D.D. Kosambi*, New Delhi: People's Publishing House.

Syed, A. (Ed.) 1983 *D.D. Kosambi on History and Society: Problems of Interpretation*, Bombay: Department of History, University of Bombay.

Thapar, Romila 1980 'The Contribution of D.D. Kosambi to Indology', *The Journal of the Asiatic Society of Bombay*, Volume 52-53, (1977-78 New Series, but apparently published in or after 1980 since this paper is based on a lecture delivered at the Society in Bombay on 29th December 1980).

Chapter six

Subaltern consciousness and populism: two approaches in the study of social movements in India

The sociology of social movements is a growing edge of the discipline in more recent decades. However, studying tribal and peasant revolts or movements was a dominant tradition both in the history and in the ethnography of India for quite some time. The pioneering accounts on the Bhumij revolts and the Kol insurrection in Chotanagpur by J.C. Jha,[1] Kalikankar Datta's work on the Santal insurrection,[2] B.B. Kling's study of the 'Blue Mutiny[3]—the indigo disturbances (1859-62)—in Bengal, and Ravinder Kumar's on the Deccan riots (1875),[4] come to mind almost immediately. The tradition continued even thereafter. Studies on the Tanabhagat or the Birsa Munda and his movement,[5] the Rampa rebellion of 1924 and of course Sunil Sen's study[6] of the sharecroppers' struggle in Bengal must also be mentioned additionally. Similarly, studies by Majid Siddiqi[7] and Kapil Kumar[8] on the agrarian/peasant revolt led by Baba Ramchandra in Pratapgarh and Faizabad districts of Oudh have notably continued the same trend in more recent years. The list is only illustrative and not exhaustive.

If one looks at the approaches or frameworks of analysis in the studies mentioned above, then, barring Ravinder Kumar, who has used the framework of class analysis meaningfully in studying the anti-moneylender Deccan riots, most of the other pioneering studies are either pure histories or ethnographies of tribal/peasant protest movements. Rarely have the researchers gone into conceptual discussions and they have not found it necessary to use or examine any of the prevailing theoretical-analytical paradigms.

Notable exceptions to this are the studies by Siddiqi,[9] Kapil Kumar,[10] Gyanendra Pandey,[11] and Dhanagare[12] who have started an important debate on the precise linkage between the peasantry and the Indian National Congress, and Gandhi in particular. However, the middle peasant thesis (like that of Eric Wolf and Hamza Alavi)[13] and Barrington Moore's[14] hypothesis on the role of commercial agriculture as a factor conducive for peasant mobilization have been thoroughly examined by only a few of the studies referred to above.[15] This is not to underrate the value of other studies. Most of them have brought to light enormous source material which otherwise would have remained unknown to the present generation of social scientists. Their accounts are the most authentic reconstructions of the peasant revolts in India in the 1920s and 1930s, but most of them belong basically to narrative history or ethnography. Some of them, like Siddiqi, Pandey and Kapil Kumar, do identify and probe the historical conditions that facilitated the progressive development of consciousness of the insurgent peasantry or tribals who were the main actors of those movements. However, barring exceptions, such studies seldom transcend specificity and are rarely inclined to get into questions of theory and generality as if they are irrelevant to the history and sociology of social movements.

Only one example of this tendency should suffice to stress the point. Suresh Singh's work[16] on the Birsa Munda movement, which has produced abundant evidence of the strong millenarian elements in the Birsaite movement, makes no reference to the concept of 'millenium' at all.[17] To a certain extent, Stephen Fuch's study on the Indian aboriginals has gone into the millenarian movements among Indian tribals under the influence of Christianity, but only superficially. Similarly, the notions of 'primitive rebels' and 'social banditry' introduced by Eric Hobsbawm,[18] have not been used fruitfully by any researcher of tribal and peasant revolts or insurgencies until Ranajit Guha and his colleagues launched the 'subaltern studies' approach in a big way. Getting immersed in the depths of the micro-level reality and not rising above it in order to enter the realm of theorization and conceptualiaztion was the tendency characteristic of the mainstream sociology and social anthropology as well as of history and ethnography that we in India received as a part of the imperialist legacy for the social sciences. The need to identify and evaluate the relevance or such paradigms, at least the neglected ones, is therefore an urgent task that cannot be overemphasized.

The purpose of this paper is to draw attention to only two of these potentially useful analytical paradigms for studying tribal/ethnic movements or peasant revolts in India. These approaches have unfortunately remained neglected at least by the mainstream sociology and social anthropology in India. It is high time we took cognizance of them and entered into paradigmatic dialogue.

Subaltern studies

An important approach to the study of tribal/peasant movements has been enunciated by Ranajit Guha and his historian colleagues in India and abroad. Broadly designated as 'subaltern historiography', this approach seeks to restore a balance by highlighting the role of the politics of the people as against elite politics played in Indian history. Thus, 'elite' and 'people' are viewed as binary domains to constitute a structural dichotomy. Adherents to this appraoch argue that the elitist historiography, whether of the neo-colonialist or of the neo-nationalist variety, has always overstated the part the elite has played in building Indian nationalism, but it has failed to acknowledge, far less properly interpret, the contributions made by the people (masses) on their own, independently of the elite.[19] Parallel to the domain of elite politics there always existed throughout the colonial period another domain of Indian politics in which the principal actors were not the dominant groups of the indigenous society but the 'subaltern' classes and groups constituting the masses of the labouring population and the intermediate strata in the town and country—the people.[20]

Subaltern historiography treats 'people' (subalternity) as an autonomous domain that originates neither from elite politics nor depends on them. Therefore, whereas the mobilization in the domain of elite politics is achieved vertically, in that of subaltern politics it is achieved horizontally. Guha, however, does admit that given the diversity of its social composition, the ideological element in the subaltern domain is not uniform in quality and density and at times such diversities lead to pursuit of sectional interests, economistic diversions as well as sectarian splits that tend to undermine the horizontal alliances in this domain. Therefore, Guha also clarifies that the two domains have not been sealed off from each other but often overlapped mainly because the elite domain always tried to mobilize and integrate them but primarily to fight for elite objectives; however, the subaltern masses managed to break away from the elite control and put their characteristic stamp on campaigns initiated by the elite groups.[21]

The whole thrust of subaltern historiography is on reconstructing 'the other history', i.e., history of people's politics and movements and their attempts to make their own history. As a brilliant demonstration of how the 'other history' could be constructed Guha has offered us a study of the peasant insurgency in colonial India.[22] Somehow, in the din over the polemical aspects of the concept of 'subalternity', the deeper insights and distinct analytical approach Guha's own study has offered have been lost sight of. The study provides us with a useful framework for studying social movements in general and tribal/peasant insurgencies in particular. It is, of course, anchored in subaltern historiography for understanding the complex phenomena of peasant or ethnic protest movements—or at least a significant part of it—in contemporary India. It is one of those serious pieces of social science scholarship which has raised many theoretical and methodological issues that must not only be acknowledged but also debated seriously.

While analyzing the tribal and peasant insurgencies in colonial India, Guha makes no secret of the fact that his approach to the study of social movements basically forms a part of the general tradition of scientific Marxism—but a variant of it quite obviously deduced from Gramsci's formulations[23] that are refreshingly original and hence intellectually very stimulating. With all the candidness that is often associated with a Marxist, Guha believes that the task of historiography is to interpret the past in order to change the present world and that such a change involves a radical transformation of consciousness. He, therefore, warns social scientists and activists not to view peasant or tribal insurgents merely as 'objects' of history but to treat them as 'makers' of their own history—endowed with a transformative consciousness of their own.

In spelling out his 'subaltern' approach Guha naturally hits out at the conventional discourses on peasant/tribal insurgencies which hitherto have served in the colonialist historiography as merely an apology for 'law and order'. Those attempts to understand insurgent movements were simply aimed at 'counter-insurgency' to prevent their occurrence in future. The sense of history was thus converted by the conventional discourses into an element of 'administrative concern'.[24] At the same time Guha is equally critical of orthodox Marxist historiography for its failure to recognize the role of pure spontaneity in history. His target is clearly set on all those recent peasant studies (i.e., studies on peasant movements including revolts or insurgencies) which have emphasized 'organization', 'leadership', and 'ideology' as the key elements in the formation of rebels' consciousness and have tended to treat the insurgencies as 'pre-political' phenomena.[25] Guha observes that those who do not recognize the first glimmer of consciousness in apparently spontaneous and unstructured movements of the peasant or tribal masses and often brand them as 'pre-political', commit a serious error of judgement.

Are the peasant and tribal insurgencies in colonial India 'pre-political' or 'political' phenomena? To Guha the term 'pre-political' is as misleading as it is value-laden; it helps us the least in understanding the experience of such movements in colonial India. Tribal or peasant insurgencies have to be understood in the backdrop of the attempts of the colonial state to revitalize landlordism and to promote parasitic landlordism. The peasant and tribal tenantry rebelled against *sarkari, sahukari*, and *zamindari* oppression to which they were subjected. The uprisings of Bhumij, the Kol insurrection, the Santal revolt of 1855, the indigo disturbances of 1859-62, and the Deccan riots of 1875 in the nineteenth century come to mind almost immediately. The subaltern insurgents were then trying to break and destroy the then existing structure of power relationships.[26] Hence, the insurgents' action was no less political than the politics of the liberal reformist struggles of the 'no-rent' or 'no-tax' variety under the banner of the Congress or the Left-wing insurrectionary struggles of peasants (such as the Tebhaga or Telangana struggles) of the twentieth century in India. Guha, however, admits that none of the basic elements (i.e., leadership, aims, programmes and ideology) of the insurgencies of the 1793-1900 period (roughly from the Rangpur uprising to the Birsa Munda movement) could compare in *maturity and sophistication* with those of the *historically more advanced movements of the twentieth century*[27] (emphasis added). Thus, he too accepts the fact that the twentieth century movements of the peasantry and tribals have been qualitatively different and decisively *more advanced*—which hopefully refers to the level of consciousness, organization and ideologial articulation. If the argument is that the difference between the two sets of movements that we designate 'pre-political' and 'political' is to be seen essentially in relative degrees and not in absolute terms, then one can have little disagreement with Guha. But if he is suggesting that such a qualitative difference does not exist then it is difficult to agree with him. Those who treat the nineteenth century peasant or tribal insurgencies as 'pre-political phenomena' would also agree that just because the sporadic and spasmodic revolts failed to rise above localism, sectarianism and ethnicity does not take away from them either their essentially political character, or their significance in history.

Guha's main objective in studying insurgencies of the colonial period is to show how patterns of subordination and insubordination have run on parallel tracks throughout the colonial history of India, and how affirmation of domination or resistance, or insurgency and counter-insurgency have reinforced each other. It is not difficult to see the influence of Hobsbawm's works[28] and also of George Rude[29] on Guha's study. Guha has abstracted certain common forms and general ideas in the rebels' consciousness. These forms—in all six—are: 'negation' (implying formation of negative identity), 'ambiguity', 'modality', 'solidarity', 'transmission' and 'territoriality'. He draws his evidence to construct these paradigmatic forms from various peasant and tribal movements of the 1793-1900 period studied extensively by anthropologists, ethnographers and historians. Since Guha's framework has a heuristic value in studying a variety of tribal/ethnic or peasant movements it is necessary to deal with these six forms at some length.

The first elementary form of peasant or insurgent tribal consciousness is 'negation' which connotes that the rebel's identity is first found by him not in his own properties, but by the diminution and negation of those of his superiors. Such a negativity may not be a fully developed class consciousness; but taking a cue from Gramsci again, Guha regards negativity as the first glimmer of that consciousness.[30] Accompanied by the ability to discriminate friends from foes, negation often results in selective violence only against the perceived enemies. The *jaqueries* in France, the peasant wars in Germany[31] and also the famous Luddite machine-breaking riots or Captain Swing type movements in England during the early phase of the Industrial Revolution[32] portrayed the same negativity in which violence spread by analogy and transference.[33] In the Indian context, peasant and tribal insurgents often reversed or rejected the homological relations in feudal society; all traditional forms of respect, dress, writing, language-styles, etc., were turned upside down. These were insignia symbolic of the exclusive preserve of feudal monarchies, nobility from which the subaltern were always debarred. The rebel's defiance of these structural rules (acts of inversion) was thus a negative assertion of his identity and consciousness.[34]

The second form—'ambiguity'—in Guha's scheme draws on the basic difference between 'crime' and 'insurgency', although the two have often been used synonymously in colonial historiography. To Guha, crime tends to be an individualistic or small group-oriented, but secretive or conspiratorial, action. In contrast, insurgency has a mass character which manifests publicly. The two acts derive from two different codes of violence, but since in the overt form the acted violence may be similar, there is an ambiguity in violence as an internal or integral part of insurgency.

'Modality'—the next elementary aspect—is a logical extension of the public character of tribal or peasant insurgencies. Drawing on the episodes of the Pabna riots (1873), the Santal *hool* (1855) and the Deccan riots (1875), Guha shows how by electing 'rebel-nawabs' and the like, the insurgents truly searched for an alternative source of authority. It is often formalized by the geneal body of insurgents through ritual presentation of *nazranas* which marks validation and sacrilization of the rebel violence as a public service.[35]

In the actual autonomous process of mobilization, the pull of primordial loyalties or sentiments of kinship, ethnic community ties and co-residence often play a significant part. However, Guha has stressed the fact that 'it was only rarely that the mobilization of an insurgent peasantry or a tribal group adopted so explicitly a religious form in colonial India as one might expect'.[36] The observation—both sweeping and hasty—is actually falsified by Guha's own evidence on the 1857 Mutiny and of course on the Birsa Munda movement which clearly showed the religious overtones of their agrarian distress coupled with ethnic identity.[37] Moreover, if Guha had carefully looked at the Moplah insurgencies from 1830 to 1921[38] then he would have certainly qualified his claim regarding the strikingly 'secular' modality of such peasant or tribal uprisings.

It is true that no narrowly conceived economic interpretations can possibly explain some of the forms in which the rebel activity manifests. Guha has asserted that when subaltern sections resorted to burning, wrecking and destroying, the considerations of economic gain did not figure very prominently. But can this modality (relating to non-economic orientation) be stated as a general law? Is economic rationality absent totally in the insurgent's action and is it always overwhelmed by motives of power as exclusively as Guha suggests? How else do we account for the umpteen instances of plunder of goods and looting of cash by the Kols in Chotanagpur and by the Santals, the details of which have been furnished by Guha himself?[39] The plunder and loot are far from incidental acts of negativity or inversion but can certainly be tinged by it. Tribal or peasant insurgents do not simply aim at destroying the cultural insignia and symbols of power but they also care for economic gains if and when opportunities come their way. In glorifying and sentimentalizing the insurgents' actions, as Guha does, it is not always necessary to deny them their normal attributes of robust practical wisdom and economic rationality as the colonialist historiography often did. Quite paradoxically, Guha is caught in the same fallacy that his subaltern approach aims at demolishing.

In contrast to plunder and destruction as a modality, killings and bloodshed tend to be a rarer phenomenon and hence must not be treated as the principal feature of insurgent behaviour. Guha argues: 'It is in fact counter-insurgency which makes killings as its principal modality.' The rarity of bloodshed in peasant or tribal insurgencies has been attributed by Guha not to their compassion but to their failure to overcome the inhibitions of the old semi-feudal culture and the spiritual conditions of their subalternity.[40]

'Solidarity'—the next form in which the peasant or tribal insurgent's self-consciousness manifests itself—signifies separation of his own identity from that of his enemies. Although this form overlaps with negativity considerably, Guha has made two important points here. First, the quality of 'collective consciousness' (*a la* Durkheim) varies from one phase of insurgency to another. Secondly, class 'solidarity' and other solidarities (i.e., those emerging from ethnic, religious, caste or filial ties) are not mutually exclusive; rather 'these overlap as they did in most of the peasant uprisings or ethnic movements before 1900 because the dye of the traditional culture had not yet washed off the peasant/ethnic consciousness'. This is what Guha characterizes as the duplex character of insurgency[41] in which sometimes class and religion are intertwined (e.g., as in the Moplah uprisings) and sometimes ethnicity and class identities get fused as is best illustrated by the case of the Birsa Munda movement.[42] In fact, Guha goes a step forward and argues that the Kol and Birsa rebellions stand apart from the rest of the tribal uprisings in the nineteenth century in that class solidarity had triumphed over ethnicity in those cases more decisively than in any other tribal uprising. Of course, Suresh Singh, whose evidence has been used by Guha, has himself not attempted a clear-cut analysis of the Birsaite movement. Thus, Guha claims that the rebel consciousness in those instances projected well beyond the sense of tribe or caste.[43]

The solidarity of the rebel peasant or tribal manifests in chastisement of traitors. 'Active collaboration is sired by insurgency no less than is rebel solidarity itself. Thus, solidarity and collaboration (betrayal) close on each other in a figure of perfect symmetry. The rebel's hostility to traitor is thus an articulation of the rebel's own class consciousness',[44] which is similar to the identity being defined negatively.

In 'transmission' as a form/aspect of peasant or tribal insurgency, Guha deals essentially with the patterns of spread of insurgency. Through iconic and symbolic signs or even rumours, other subaltern sections/groups are also contacted and drawn into uprising. Whether the rebels organize prayer meetings, beat their drums, flutes or horns, distribute branches of *sal* trees, or a fiery torch, or whether they distribute *chapatis, tel* (oil) or *sindur* (vermillion powder), all these were the most effective instruments of this transmission in the Kol, the Santal and the Birsaite movements, in the Sepoy Mutiny of 1857, and also in the Moplah rebellion of 1921.[45] What is significant is that in this transmission by verbal codes or through visual signs, the ideology of class struggle is invariably mediated by religion because Guha believes that the politics of rebellion or tribal insurgencies are almost always expressed in sacred idioms as they are very effective in arousing mass support.[46]

Lastly, 'territoriality' is that aspect or form of peasant/tribal consciousness in which insurgents get bound by blood ties (consanguinity) on the one hand and by local bond (contiguity) on the other. A sense of belongingness to a common lineage and to a shared habital overlap with one another. Thus, ethnic space and physical space notions are constituents of territoriality. Guha has stressed the fact that even this consciousness has often transcended the limits of ties of either blood or habitat or both. Therefore, the 1857 Mutiny could spread far beyond the heartland of the Doab region as well as Oudh.[47] In this context Guha has criticized S.C. Roy and many other anthropologists who failed to see through the anti-colonial content of the tribal revolts or peasant movements in India and who thereby have helped to perpetuate the myth that tribal/peasant insurgency was nothing more than a demonstration of ethnic antagonism against the *diku* (i.e., outsider)[48] and that peasant movements were nothing but 'disturbances' that created law and order problems for the colonial administration. But in one sense, the ethnic antagonism—expressed in idioms like *diku*—is also a way of redefining 'imperialism' as 'internal colonialism': a point missed completely by Guha.

The common forms or patterns of peasant/tribal insurgents' consciousness are made up not only of elements and tendencies which are mutually consistent but also those which clash and conflict with one another. Guha does not visualize the common form in which the rebels' consciousness manifests as a generality that is external to the subject or that is a *sui generis* phenomenon, nor is it any abstract quality of insurgency discovered by pure abstraction and reflection. Rather, it is what permeates and includes in it everything particular. Hence, Guha's framework consists of 'abstracted elementary forms' that are firmly rooted in the concrete foundation of facts drawn from the nineteenth century peasant/tribal insurgencies. Therefore, the impact of Durkheim on Guha's analytical framework is more apparent than real. Like formal sociologists (George Simmel and others) Guha does not fall into the trap of reification—a standard error in any formal analysis. Instead his sight is fixed on the insurgent Kols, Santals and Birsaite movements; it is these rebels' consciousness which Guha has analyzed and it is the deep historical meaning of their insurgencies in colonial India to which his study draws our attention.

The subaltern approach, at least the form in which Guha has demonstrated its use in his own study[49] of peasant insurgencies, as stated earlier, draws heavily on Emile Durkheim's notion of 'elementary forms', or George Simmel's concept of 'forms' of interaction. In substance, however, the subaltern studies approach as it developed in India clearly represents a synthesis of four major streams within contemporary Marxism: (i) First and the most obvious of these is Gramscian Marxism which emphasizes the role of pure spontaneity of the action of subaltern masses in history in general and under a hegemonic state in particular. For theoretical justification, conceptual/analytical tools, and also for abstractions of general explanation, the subaltern approach draws obviously on Gramsci. (ii) No less obvious is the influence of Trotskyite-Marxism, particularly in terms of consciousness (i.e., necessary as opposed to contingent consciousness). Guha's subaltern studies approach treats consciousness the way Trotsky did. For Trotsky, objective theoretical positions reigned supreme and these must be judged objectively, rather than shifting them pragmatically, as the Stalinist politicians often did, by twisting their theoretical pronouncements guided by personal power ambitions or political motivations.[50] Following Trotsky then, the subaltern approach to history considers the role of party, strategies and tactics as important, no doubt, but not as prior to 'necessary consciousness'. (iii) The third Marxist stream which Guha's own approach draws inspiration from is represented by Eric Hobsbawm, George Rude and E.P. Thompson, who through their studies,[51] have shown the indispensability of the material force and actors of history. (iv) And finally, in terms of the directions in which subaltern struggles develop, or the forms in which they manifest, Guha and his associates have clearly tended to model their arguments on the lines indicated by the 1968 Paris uprisings (i.e., the massive student and youth protest that finally brought the downfall of Charles de Gaulle), the Latin American movements—particularly the experience of Che Guevera in Bolivia and the like. It is a blend of these four traditions in contemporary Marxism that Guha's subaltern studies approach to history represents.

The 'subaltern studies' approach earned critics as fast as it gained a following, particularly among young historians from both India and abroad, though not so much among other social scientists. These historians have focused their attention on peasants, workers and other subaltern elements, in an attempt to show how their protests have been spontaneous and traditional and yet far more radical in their methods of resistance, sometimes even in their goals, than the elite and middle-class dominated nationalist movement in India was. Above all, in conformity with Ranajit Guha's contention, these studies, the results of which are now available in a series of five volumes,[52] also argue that such spontaneous movements were independent of the nationalist leadership which often tried to control them if possible, or even to suppress and subvert them whenever necessary.[53]

Critics of the 'subaltern studies' approach have attacked precisely the whole notion of 'autonomy' of the subaltern consciousness. Irfan Habib and many others have questioned the validity of such an attempt to study subaltern groups and their protest movements in isolation from other parallel political processes. A struggle or a protest movement that appears to be autonomous, is in reality preceded by several changes in the consciousness of its principal participants. Such changes often emanate from wider political processes, including the elite politics which the subaltern approach followers have decried. In the Indian context the interface between the national movement led by the Indian National Congress and the grass-root level protests and resistance movements is too significant to be ignored, because the latter was a prime source of ideas for the former.[54]

Another major difficulty with the subaltern studies approach pertains to the lack of precise meaning and scope of the concept of 'subalternity' as an analytical category. In a separate note on the term by Guha[55] he admits that the composition of this category is not homogeneous. The term is more residual in its connotation as it includes practically all non-elite sections of the people. Guha treats the lowest strata of the rural gentry, impoverished landlords, rich and upper middle peasants as all belonging to the category of 'people' or 'subaltern classes'. But then he has left it to individual researchers to investigate, identify and determine the specific nature of subalternity by situating it historically. With this rider it should be possible to consider *adivasis* (tribals), untouchables or *dalits*, sharecroppers, and agricultural labourers, as well as other marginalized sections with specific ethnic, non-class characteristics (caste, religion, clan, language or regional identity of a minority group) as 'subaltern classes'. But then by no stretch of imagination can the class outlook and interests of these immiserized and marginalized groups be compatible, let alone identical, with those of the lowest strata of rural gentry, the rich and upper-middle peasantry whom Guha treats as the ideal components of 'subalternity'.

More importantly, the subaltern studies approach to historiography in a way confines itself preferentially to the colonial period, though not all the adherents strictly do so. In addition to this, at least by implication, the approach is applicable only to those mass mobilizations which took on the insurgent character, and hence it is inapplicable to those tribal/peasant or any other protest movements which were not truly insurgent in character. This again, by implication, severely restricts the scope of Gramscian formulations. If, however, members of the 'subaltern studies' group (or maybe school) insist that the concept should be used for studying only the insurgent responses of the people during the colonial period, then the approach excludes all those ethnic/tribal, peasant, or any other protest movements which are not necessarily insurgent in character but which can be called as 'revolutions of rising expectations'.

If the contents of the 'subaltern studies' series are subjected to a closer scrutiny, then not all contributors have conformed to the definition specified in Guha's initial note. For example, Arvind Das,[56] in his account of the East Champaran Kisan Sabha in Jhakia and the landgrab movement in Bihar in general, has essentially dealt with the agrarian movements of the poor and landless peasants in the 1960s and 1970s. In the context of Masaurhi (1970-75) again it is the struggle of the agricultural labourers of Harijan castes that he has discussed.[57] There are many other studies on agricultural labourers' or jute-workers' struggles which, strictly speaking, do not fit into the rigid definitional ambit of 'subaltern classes' as drawn by Guha. Another example is David Hardiman's study[58] on the Devi movement among the tribals of Gujarat, which too does not fit into the 'subaltern studies' strait-jacket.

Even if we accept 'subalternity' as a generic conceptual category, which is to be defined and situated historically (which would theoretically make it an open category to include practically any class or stratum of a society), still other ambiguities remain. The most important one relates to the proximity of this concept to 'insurgencies'. Some of the studies in the subaltern series have, of course, dealt with movements—protests/mobilizations—which are not insurgent in character. Since neither in its scope of applicability nor in terms of the basic properties of 'subaltern' behaviour the concept of 'subalternity' suggests any specific boundaries, its status as a scientific concept remains rather doubtful.

In our opinion, more useful than the concept of 'subalternity' is Ranajit Guha's framework consisting of six forms or aspects of insurgents' consciousness for all those interested in studying social movements in general, and ethnic/tribal and peasant movements in particular. The value of Guha's paradigmatic forms remains undiminished regardless of whether we accept or eliminate the 'subaltern' concept from his framework. The only limitation of Guha's paradigm lies in its restricted applicability or suitability for studying only those movements which took on an insurgent character, because his 'elementary aspects' spell out precisely the basic properties of the insurgent's action. A large number of ethnic/tribal movements, or more recent farmers' movements in India from the 1950s, are left out because they did not develop necessarily along the insurgent syndrome.

The identity formations of ethnic/tribal groups, peasantry, or even among minorities and their political expressions in contemporary India present a wide spectrum. They range from the nativist movements like the Shiv Sena in Maharashtra (which is militant but not radical),[59] or movements for assertion of regional/sub-regional identities such as for a separate Vidarbha[60] or Telengana[61] state on the one hand, to the Jharkhand movement in the Chotanagpur district of Bihar,[62] and many other 'sons of the soil' movements[63] which have sometimes taken on insurgent, militant or even terrorist forms, but have most of the time sought to pursue their demands within the constitutional framework of India and by accepting its legitimacy as well as the liberal democratic means. Some of these movements, or at least a fraction of them, have raised secessionist demands questioning the very legitimacy of India as a nation-state. However, most of these contemporary movements come fairly close to what T. Di Tella has called 'the revolutions of rising expectations' which are often unleashed by developmental imbalances resulting from the modernization process in the Third World. The most striking example of this is the farmers' movements that have gathered momentum in different parts of India since the mid-seventies to demand remunerative prices for farm produce. Ideologues of these movements argue that while agricultural productivity has risen phenomenally as a result of the Green Revolution—and its subsidized inputs—agricultural profitability has declined sharply due to non-remunerative prices. The Bharatiya Kisan Union movement in Punjab and Uttar Pradesh, the Shetkari Sanghatana in Maharashtra, or the Rajya Rayatha Sangh in Karnataka and the like belong essentially to this category of protest movements. Ernesto Laclau[64] has tried to develop a proper framework for studying such movements, which he characterizes as 'populist movements'. In our view, we in India ought to examine Laclau's attempt to theorize on 'populism' more seriously, since it is directly relevant for understanding the complex phenomena of contemporary movements—whether farmers', ethnic, tribal or regional.

Interpretations of populism

Laclau has mentioned four basic approaches to an interpretation of populism. For the first approach, populism is a typical expression of a determinate social class and hence it is both a movement and an ideology at the same time. For example, the Russian Narodnik populism in the nineteenth century was no more than a peasant ideology; the North American populism in 1895 was an ideology and mobilization typical of a society of small farmers opposed to urban life and big business; and the more recent Latin American mobilization of urban masses is an ideological-political expression of a petty bourgeoisie or of marginal sectors.[65] In this approach a type of populism is established by its class base or class combination.

The second conception of populism treats it with a theoretical nihilism, as if the concept is devoid of any content. For example, Peter Worsley[66] argues that it is difficult to specify common crucial attributes that are present in all movements that are usually characterized as 'populist'. Hence, populism is not an analytical category but a datum of experience.[67] But despite its conceptual imprecision or indefinition, populism has gained more and more respectability in the social sciences.

According to the third approach, the difficulties in the term could be overcome by restricting it to characterization of ideology only, and not of a movement. As an ideology, the main properties of 'populism' are: (i) its ingrained hostility to the *status quo*; (ii) mistrust of traditional politicians; (iii) appeal to the people or masses and not to specific classes as such; and finally (iv) its anti-intellectualism.[68] Such a peculiar ideological nexus gets formed and adopted by social movements that differ widely in their social origins as well as in their aspirations. Though useful, this approach helps only in studying or describing the 'form' but not the content of social movements, because a simple characterization of populist elements or behavioural forms would say nothing of the role such a movement plays in a determinate social formation in a spatio-temporal context.[69]

The fourth conception of populism is derived from functionalist theory. Its argument, to put it in its simplest form, would run as follows: when aspirations, guided by culturally defined goals, are kept constantly rising, but are not matched by adequate institutional means to fulfil them, such a situation creates different forms of adaptation on the part of individuals to the social structure. All forms of adaptation other than 'conformist' behaviour are considered in the functionalist paradigm as 'deviations' or aberrations.[70] Populism in this functionalist perspective would be seen as an aberrant phenomenon produced by 'the asynchronism of the processes of transition from a traditional to an industrial society'.[71]

Drawing from the comparative assessments of the European and Latin American experience, G. Germani has formulated a theory of populism.[72] Germani also treats populism as a product of a transitional stage between traditional and industrial societies in which features of advanced stages correspond to a backward stage. This constitutes 'asynchronism'. Co-existence of these two would mean that modernization in one will provoke change in the others, but not necessarily in a modern direction. Populism combines these two opposite tendencies in two forms—the demonstration effect and the fusion effect. The former refers to widespread diffusion of habits, mentalities and styles that correspond to a more advanced stage in backward areas. In the latter form (i.e., the fusion effect), ideologies and attitudes corresponding to the advanced stage are reinterpreted in a backward context, which in turn reinforce the traditional features. Populism, therefore, seeks to achieve mobilization and integration, change and *status quo* at the same time.[73] In other words, populist movements are anti-*status quoist* and *status quoist* at the same time. And this blend of change as well as stability orientations, when pursued simultaneously through ideology, constitutes 'populism'.

Another Latin American scholar, Torcuato Di Tella has defined 'populism' as a political movement which enjoys the support of the masses of the urban working class and/or peasantry, but which does not result from the autonomous organizational power of either of these two sectors. It is also supported by non-working class or non-peasant sections upholding an anti-*status quo* ideology. Hence, to Di Tella, social classes are present in populism but not necessarily as classes. A peculiar ideology achieves the separation of the class nature of participants and their forms of political expression, which, in our view, is truly happening in the phenomenal growth of farmers' movements all over India in more recent years. Populism in this sense is the 'revolution of rising expectations' responsible for the asynchronism.[74] Hence, three essential features of populism are stressed by Di Tella: (i) an elite committed to mobilization of masses appears on the scene—an elite that is imbued with an anti-*status quo* ideology; (ii) mass mobilization generated by rising expectations; and (iii) an ideology with a widespread appeal. What is, however, important is that the roots of these three features are sought in the transition or 'asynchronism'.[75]

In the ultimate analysis, although classes appear in populist movements but not as classes, the meaning of the ideological elements identified with populism has to be sought in the social structure. And these structures refer back again to the class nature of populist movements. Di Tella's formulations thus suggest that to a higher degree of development would correspond more of a 'class' and less of a 'populist' organization. This amounts to saying that populist experiences or movements are likely to be less frequent in capitalist societies than in peripheral countries due to different levels of development. Laclau has, however, contested this point since 'developed-underdeveloped', 'traditional-modern' or 'agrarian-industrial' dichotomies are used by Di Tella as prior paradigms for defining 'populism'.[76]

The confusion over the concept of 'populism' is largely due to two opposing tendencies among analysts of such movements or populist phenomena: (i) either to specify the class nature of specific populist movements, and then to treat class contradictions as the fundamental structural moment for discerning political and ideological features; or (ii) to differentiate between class determination of superstructures and the form of existence of classes at the level of these superstructures. Orthodox Marxism theorizes superstructures as reflections of production, and makes class consciousness the basic constitutive movement of class. Gramsci, and following him Laclau, abandon this reductionist way of defining classes as antagonistic poles of production relations. They argue that: (i) classes exist at the ideological and political level in a process of articulation and not of reduction; (ii) that articulation requires non-class contents—interpellations and contradictions which constitute the raw material on which class ideological practices operate. Thus, the ideology of the dominant class, precisely because it is dominant, interpellates not just the members of that class but also members of the dominated classes, and thereby their potential antagonism is neutralized; (ii) the levels of political and ideological superstructures must be conceived in the form of articulation and not of reduction; (iv) therefore, populist discourse refers primarily to 'people' or masses, though class as historical agent of the people's interests is very much present there; and finally (v) people/power bloc contradictions are distinct from a class contradiction. Populist movements express primarily the former,[77] and they arise in a specific ideological domain. The dialectical tension between the 'people' and 'classes' determines the form of ideology.[78] The Gramscian impact on Laclau's theoretical formulations on 'populism' is too evident to need any further elaboration of his analytical framework.

The potential

Having looked at the 'subaltern studies' approach and 'populism' as a conceptual tool it is necessary to assess their potential as useful frameworks for studying social movements—including ethnic/tribal, and peasant movements in India. To us, heuristically more significant than the concept of 'subalternity' in the alternative approach to historiography advocated by Ranajit Guha, are the six paradigmatic forms (suggested by him) in which insurgent consciousness manifests. For studying protest movements of peasantry and ethnic/tribal groups in general, and their insurgencies in particular, Guha's forms are invaluable; they suggest what questions a researcher ought to ask while studying any insurgent phenomenon, and how to interpret and interconnect seemingly disparate sets of data in order to reconstruct the nature of consciousness of the insurgent people whom one has chosen to study. This framework consisting of Guha's six paradigmatic forms, could be usefully employed in studying ethnic/tribal and peasant movements, but mainly of the insurgent variety, without making much *ado* of the concept of 'subalternity' *per se.* It is not being suggested here that the concept ought to be discarded outright. However, its extensive usage in specific historical contexts inquired into by the contributors to the *Subaltern Studies* series has not in any way minimized either the extent of ambiguities it is ridden with or the polemics associated with it. On the contrary, it has become increasingly difficult to use the term 'subalternity' with conceptual precision or a common meaning structure as the body of research literature on subaltern issues keeps growing.

Guha's paradigmatic forms too, though useful, have some obvious limitations. They are useful for studying insurgent movements only. Naturally, non-insurgent protest movements would remain outside the pale of his paradigm. Moreover, these forms in themselves are not fixed or determinate, and would require continuous renewal in the light of fresh research material; finally these forms in themselves do not constitute an explanation as to why a given movement or insurgency assumes certain of these forms and not others.

It is here that the concept of 'populism', and the framework that Laclau and other Latin American scholars have suggested for studying 'populist movements', could possibly provide us with directions for inquiries into contemporary peasant/farmers' movements, ethnic/tribal movements, or movements for assertion of regional, ethnic or minority identities, which are becoming less and less insurgent in character and are acquiring the form of 'populism', i.e., 'revolution of rising expectations'. In these movements 'people' or masses and not 'classes' seem to be getting united against the *status quo* establishment, and such a unity or solidarity is apparently achieved through ideology despite the presence of one or more dominant classes operating within such populist formations.

The precise linkages between masses and classes, the nature of populist ideologies and the type of inter-class unity these ideological interpellations achieve, and the role such populist movements play in a determinate social formation or in a given mode of production, are some of the issues that could be taken up for inquiry in the context of contemporary social movements—more particularly peasants'/farmers' movements or ethnic movements in India. Guha's framework of the six forms of rebel's consciousness, and Laclau's formulations on 'populism', which have regrettably remained neglected in the mainstream sociology and social anthropology of movements in India, could provide us with some directions for future inquiry.

Notes and references

1. J.C. Jha, *The Kol Insurrection of Chotanagpur*, Thacker, Spink Co., Calcutta, 1964; *The Bhumij Revolt 1832-1833* (Ganga Narain's Hungama or Turmoil), Munshiram Manoharlal, Delhi, 1967.
2. K.K. Datta, *The Santal Insurrection-1855*, University of Calcutta Press, Calcutta, 1944.
3. B.B. Kling, *The Blue Mutiny—The Indigo Disturbances in Bengal 1859-1862*, The University of Pennsylvania Press, Philadelphia, 1966.
4. Ravinder Kumar, *Western India in the Nineteenth Century*, Routledge and Kegan Paul, London, 1968.
5. K. Suresh Singh, *Dust Storm and Hanging Mist—Birsa Munda and His Movement*, Firma K.L. Mukhopadhyay, Calcutta, 1966; *Birsa Munda and His Movement in Chotanagpur*, Oxford University Press, Calcutta, 1983.
6. Sunil K. Sen, *Agrarian Struggles in Bengal 1946-1947*, Peoples' Publishing House, Delhi, 1972.
7. Majid H. Siddiqi, *Agrarian Unrest in Northern India—The United Provinces, 1918-22*, Vikas Publishers, New Delhi, 1978.
8. Kapil Kumar, *Peasants in Revolt: Tenants, Landlords, Congress and the Raj in Oudh, 1886-1922*, Manohar, Delhi, 1984.
9. Majid H. Siddiqi, *op. cit.*
10. Kapil Kumar, *op. cit.*
11. Gyanendra Pandey, *The Ascendancy of the Congress in Uttar Pradesh, 1926-34: A Study in Imperfect Mobilization*, Oxford University Press, Delhi, 1978.
12. D.N. Dhanagare, *Peasant Movements in India 1920-1950*, Oxford University Press, Delhi, 1983.
13. Hamza Alavi, 'Peasants and Revolution', in Ralph Miliband (Ed.), *Socialist Register*, Merlin, London, 1965.
14. B. Moore (Jr.), *Social Origins of Dictatorship and Democracy—Lord and Peasant in the Making of the Modern World*, Paladin, London, 1969.
15. D.N. Dhanagare, *op. cit.*

16. K. Suresh Singh, *Dust Storm and Hanging Mist, op. cit.*
17. This major omission was subsequently rectified by K. Suresh Singh in the revised edition of his book (1983) published under a different title in which the millenarian ethos of the Birsa Munda's movement has been highlighted.
18. Eric Hobsbawm, *Primitive Rebels*, Manchester University Press, 1959; Bandits, Penguin, Harmondsworth, 1972.
19. Ranajit Guha (Ed.), *Subaltern Studies—Writings on South Asian History and Society*, Vol. I, Oxford University Press, Delhi, 1982, pp. 2-3.
20. *Ibid.*, p. 4.
21. *Ibid.*, pp. 5-6.
22. Ranajit Guha, *Elementary Aspects of Peasant Insurgency in Colonial India*, Oxford University Press, Delhi, 1983.
23. *Ibid.*
24. *Ibid.*, pp. 3-4.
25. See D.N. Dhanagare, *op. cit.*, and Sunil K. Sen, *op. cit.*
26. Ranajit Guha (Ed.), *Subaltern Studies*, Vol. II, *op. cit.*, p. 8.
27. *Ibid.*, p. 10.
28. Eric Hobsbawm, *op. cit.*
29. George Rude, *Crowd in History—A Study of Popular Disturbances in France and England 1730-1848*, John Wiley and Sons, New York, 1964.
30. Ranajit Guha, *op. cit.*, 1983, pp. 19-20.
31. Frederick Engels, *Present Wars in Germany*, Lawrence and Wishart, London, 1969.
32. George Rude, *op. cit.*
33. Ranajit Guha, *op. cit.*, pp. 21-26.
34. *Ibid.*, pp. 54-56, 61-64.
35. *Ibid.*, pp. 112-115.
36. *Ibid.*, p. 125.
37. Suresh Singh, *op. cit.*, pp. 39-53, pp. 198-199.
38. D.N. Dhanagare, *op. cit.*
39. Ranajit Guha, *op. cit.*, 149-151.
40. *Ibid.*, pp. 161-166.
41. Ranajit Guha, *op. cit.*, pp. 169-171.
42. K. Suresh Singh, *op. cit.*, p. 202.
43. Ranajit Guha, *op. cit.*, p. 188.
44. *Ibid.*, pp. 204-209.

45. D.N. Dhanagare, *op. cit.*
46. Ranajit Guha, *op. cit.*, pp. 227-248, p. 251.
47. *Ibid.*, pp. 280-286.
48. *Ibid.*, p. 200.
49. *Ibid.*
50. J. Areh Getty, 'Trotsky in Exile: The Founding of the Fourth International', *Soviet Studies*, Vol. XXXVIII No. 1, January 1986, pp. 24-36.
51. For example, see Hobsbawm's *Primitive Rebels* (1959) and *Bandits* (1972), Rude's *Crowd in History* (1964) and E.P. Thompson's *Making of the English Working Class.* However, it is necessary to distinguish these studies from Camus' *Rebel.*
52. Ranajit Guha (Ed.) 1982-1987, *op. cit.*
53. See Kapil Kumar, *op. cit.*
54. Irfan Habib, *Interpreting Indian History*, North- eastern Hill University Publications, Shillong, approximately 1986.
55. Ranajit Guha (Ed.), *op. cit.*, Vol. I, p. 8.
56. Arvind N. Das, *Agrarian Change from Above and from Below: Bihar 1947-78* in R. Guha (ed.), Vol II, pp. 204-214.
57. *Ibid.*, pp. 215-219.
58. David Hardiman, *The Coming of Devi*, Oxford University Press, Delhi, 1987.
59. Dipankar Gupta, *Nativism in a Metropolis—Shiv Sena Movement in Bombay*, Manohar, Delhi, 1982.
60. D.N. Dhanagare, 'Vidarbhas Separate Identity—Its Emergence in Historical Outline', *State and Society*, Vol. 6, No. 4, 1986.
61. G. Rama Reddy, *Regionalism in India—A Study of Telengana*, Concept Publishing Company, Delhi, 1979.
62. K.L. Sharma, *Caste, Class and Social Movements*, Rawat Brothers, Jaipur, 1986.
63. Myron Weiner, *Sons of the Soil*, Princeton University Press, Princeton, New Jersey, 1978.
64. Ernesto Laclau, *Politics and Ideology in Marxist Theory*, Verso Publications, London, 1979.
65. *Ibid.*
66. Peter Worsely, 'The Concept of Populism', in G. Ionescu and E. Gellner (eds.), *Populism*, London, 1970.
67. Ernesto Laclau, *op. cit.*, p. 146.
68. *Ibid.*, p. 147.

69. *Ibid.*, p. 147.
70. The best exemplification of this functionalist thesis can be found in R.K. Merton, *Social Theory and Social Structure* (1968 enlarged edition reproduced as Indian edition), Amerind, New Delhi, 1975.
71. Ernesto Laclau, *op. cit.*, p. 147.
72. For a summary of Germani's theory in English, see E. Laclau, 1979.
73. Ernesto Laclau, *op. cit.*, pp. 148-149.
74. T. Di. Tella, 'Populism and Reform in Latin America', in C. Veliz (Ed.) *Obstacles to Change in Latin America*, London, 1970 and Laclau, *op. cit.*, pp. 150-151.
75. Ernesto Laclau, *op. cit.*, 152-153.
76. *Ibid.*, p. 154.
77. *Ibid.*, p. 160-167.
78. *Ibid.*, p. 194-198.

Chapter seven

Action groups and social transformation in India: some sociological issues

The emergence of a large number of action groups who have been trying to educate, conscientize and mobilize different marginalized sections, particularly the oppressed poor, has been the most important development in India since the 1960s. These social activists or groups work mostly at the micro-level, associating and identifying themselves with the weaker sections, and through action-oriented approach contribute to the broader process of social transformation. That the rise of such activist groups also coincides with the shift in focus from 'structures' to 'change' in general and social movements in particular in Indian sociology and social anthropology is not a mere historical accident. This is evident in the sizeable growth of movement studies that could be described as a growing edge of the twin disciplines today.

It is interesting to note that even in the area of sociology of social movements, more conventional movements (like the social reform or protest movements from the early nineteenth century onwards, the freedom movement and other movements of the Indian working class as well as peasantry), attracted greater attention than some of the 'new social movements'. For example, women's movements (feminist movement), science movements (like the Kerala Shastra Sahitya Parishad), peace movements or environmentalist-ecology movements and so on, were initially ignored by sociologists. It is only after some activist groups had aroused public opinion and mobilized mass support on these issues that sociologists started taking cognizance of this new phenomenon.

Some social scientists prefer to designate these 'new movements' as 'cultural movements' since most of them are neither directly engaged in class struggles *per se*, nor are they fighting a specific class adversary as such. But still these new social movements and action groups that launched them are not totally indifferent to the need to attack and alter the past social order in which the power of the ruling class is entrenched and from which the privations of marginalized sections stem either directly or indirectly (Touraine, 1981: 96).

In the sociology of social movements, it is rather trite to stress the interrelationship between social structure and social movements on the one hand and between social movements and social change or transformation on the other. Although no two sociologists would agree as to what type or nature of mobilization could qualify itself to be termed as a social movement, the feedback linkages between structures and movements and between these and social transformation (implying structural as well as value changes) are generally accepted by most sociologists of diverse persuasions and even theoretical orientations. Studies on social movements have, therefore, tended to highlight the structural context of birth of a movement, its life-cycle, ideology, organization, leadership and class— or general social origins besides the nature of transformation that it brings about. Such studies also attempt to assess a movement's success or failure in relation to its professed aims and objectives. If such studies are aimed at broader generalizations then similar exercises are attempted within a cross-cultural or comparative historical framework.

What has, however, been missed so far in Indian sociology is the phenomenon of action groups or activist groups. The growth of numerous action groups that work at the grass-roots among tribals, rural and urban poor, *dalits*, women and similar other disadvantaged sections of Indian society, is perhaps the most striking feature of contemporary social reality in India. These activist groups have created their own spaces mostly outside the sphere of organized political parties, that is, outside the structure of power politics and also outside the institutional framework of the state.

Some action groups, however, function within this framework. These groups are variously called as social activists, action groups, voluntary agencies (VAs), non-governmental organizations (NGOs), or non-party political processes or non-political formations.

Most of these groups have emerged as reactions or responses to the socio-political crises that developed in India during the past couple of decades, of which two types that have developed since the 1960s are particularly noteworthy. First, it was becoming increasingly clear that the existing developmental strategy and practice of state-directed change left much to be desired. Masses of rural and urban poor had become increasingly immiserised whereas the elite, dominant castes and ruling classes, together with a steadily expanding urban middle class, had a substantial share in benefits and access to resources disproportionately larger than their size and contribution to the growth process. For the poor masses, the developmental process had been more of a mirage than a reality. It is no longer a rhetoric but an established fact. This crisis was generated by developmental imbalances, which were not only perceived subjectively by poorer sections but were also confirmed by objective indices and statistics on poverty, landlessness, unemployment, hunger and disease, pollution, social injustices and exploitation and atrocities on women and *dalits* and the like (Dhanagare, 1984). The second crisis is marked by the breakdown or gradual deterioration and decline of the existing structures and institutions of modern nation-states (Sheth, 1982: 1-2).

Action groups in the pre-independence period

In the pre-independence period voluntary organizations, agencies for social, cultural and economic reforms and action groups had emerged from time to time. Some functioned outside the sphere of politics of the nationalist movement and worked for spreading education and literacy; some attempted social reforms among women or among specific religious communities and the like. Others operated within the framework of the nationalist or other movements, with which they were integrated both ideologically and organizationally. These groups had diverse ideological orientations ranging from Gandhian liberal reformism to militant radicalism of the Left. The most striking feature of these groups and organizations was that they sought to be linked, either directly or indirectly, to political processes at the broader level. If these action groups challenged the legitimacy of the colonial state and imperial power, they were often assimilated or integrated with the anti-imperialist national movement. If, however, they did not question the legitimacy of the British rule *per se*, but simply aimed at 'social reform' at the non-political level, such groups received encouragement, including grants-in-aid from the colonial state. In the latter case, their cooptation in the institutional framework of the state posed little or no problem. Such groups were bound to be '*status quoist*' or conservative in their general socio-political outlook although they aimed at some reforms 'within' the structure of society and institutions.

There existed still the third category of action groups in the pre-independence period which had a Marxist or radical-leftist ideological orientation. Critical of both types of action groups, whether pro-nationalist or pro-colonial, such radical groups sprang up in different parts of India with the growth of the Communist movement and also the Socialist movement. These radical left groups were largely instrumental in building a number of trade-unions and *kisan-sabhas* at the grass-roots level (Dhanagare, 1983: 129-50).

The most noteworthy feature of the action groups of all the three types in pre-independence India was their relatively simpler polarization in political terms into pro-government and pro-nationalist camps. Equally significant was the crystallization of their ideological choices into 'Gandhian liberal reformism' versus 'radical left revolutionism' that indicated clearly distinct alternative paths for the societal transformation that they envisaged. Whether it was Mahatma Jyotiba Phuley's attempt to mobilize the *bahujan-samaj* (masses) against the hegemony of elite Brahmins in Maharashtra, or the Arya-Samajist campaign for *shuddhi* (purification of those who had been converted to other faiths), or whether it was a scavengers' union mobilized by the Peasants' and Workers' Party under Muzaffar Ahmad's leadership in Bengal, or Maharshi D.K. Karve's crusade for women's upliftment in Maharashtra, whether it was the Gandhian *swaraj-ashrams* in Gujarat which undertook constructive activities including the upliftment of Harijans, or Godavari Parulekar's work of conscientizing the Warlis in Thane district of Maharashtra—all these formed an integral part of the mainstream national movement and political processes. Although ideological differences divided them sharply, action groups in pre-independence India were not isolated, nor were they mutually insulated grass-roots level activist-enthusiasts spread out like the mosaic dots on the national canvas with no relation to one another. Rather, the wider dialogue on ends and means of the anti-imperialist movement and of the process of social transformation tied them together. Action groups were in a sense responding constantly to the broader party political processes in the country.

Contemporary action groups: types and stages of development

In contrast the action groups from the mid-1960s present a bewildering variety that defies any pattern or classification. This has, however, not deterred researchers from attempting to discern meaningful patterns in the growth of action groups in contemporary India. However, before we turn to them it is necessary to spell out what is generally understood today by the term 'action group'.

Though the terms 'action groups' and 'activist groups' are often used interchangeably, it is generally recognized that they may differ in their shades of ideological radicalism or in the extent they advocate and practise militancy in mobilizing masses as well as in the distance or proximity they maintain vis-a-vis the state and established political parties or organizations. Action groups can be defined as groups working at the micro-level, in a localized setting for and with the poor, marginalized and oppressed sections of the society—whether rural or urban. These groups educate, conscientize and organize such sections towards social action aimed at transforming their lives qualitatively. Generally, such groups operate outside the institutional framework of both the government and established political parties, but are not necessarily indifferent to them. By definition activist groups are not apolitical. Some prefer to distance themselves from the mainstream political processes and power politics and hence they are conceptualized as 'non-party political processes' or formations (e.g., Kothari, 1984a, 1984b, 1986; Sheth, 1982, 1984; Sethi, 1984); others highlight the political relevance of activities or interventions of action groups. Although such groups may consciously opt to work outside power-politics, they are and have to be aware of the relations of power in local situations where groups operate and are engaged in organizing concrete struggles to resist all forms of oppression and injustices that disadvantaged sections are subjected to. Most action groups are, therefore, politically conscious of the implications of their struggles for local power structures.

Some action groups, however, may engage themselves in linking these micro-level struggles with broader (macro-level) processes and extend that consciousness in order to understand and explain local problems in the wider context of national and international systems of hegemony and exploitations. In such cases the ultimate solutions of problems at the local level are visualized only in systemic changes rather than in intra-system reforms. Other groups simply confine themselves to local situations. To them, delinking local from regional, national or trans-national politico-economic systems is necessary for self-assertion, efficacy and success, though in a limited measure, at the micro-level. Such micro-level groups tend to be more pragmatic and down-to-earth in their approach. They believe in combating concrete problems with concrete solutions and not in diffusing them by stretching the prognosis of reality to the level of ideological abstractions or philosophization, often incomprehensible to the masses with whom they work.

At this stage it would be useful to understand the precise interface or relationship between action groups and social movements at the conceptual level. Action groups can be initiators of social movements, but not necessarily their customary agents, instruments or carriers. A social movement, once institutionalized and routinized, may operate through already formed groups, parties, trade unions, organizations and similar units. When organizations become substitutes for movements, social movements find it increasingly difficult to remain aloof from political processes and institutional framework of the state power. As Alan Touraine (1981: 157) states:

> A social movement is an unstable balancing between institutionalization of that movement and critical action against order, hence between a pressure group of interests on the one hand and a party or an armed force ready to take over power on the other hand.

An action group which initiates the mobilization process and acts as a catalyst of a social movement may also become its principal sheet-anchor when that movement moves in the direction of institutionalization representing a broader zone of social and political action. But some action groups may dissociate or withdraw from the movement when it displays an inclination towards institutionalization. Initiators, thus, may themselves become dissenters, or splinter groups and may choose to remain militants without movements or organizations. Action groups in such cases are intervention groups of militants or activists for whom only a grass-roots level involvement with people in their real-life situation and actual struggles is more meaningful and purposeful than ideologically-oriented political struggles at the macro-level. They may not thus be interested in the broader level systemic changes through social movements. Conceptually, therefore, social movement and action groups are separable, though empirically there usually exists some relationship between the two, though not a determinate one.

Critical studies on action groups have suggested certain typologies or schemes for their classification, or identified stages of their development. One such attempt speaks of three stages—social welfarism, radical nationalism and finally, the stage of socialist orientation (John, 1982: 1-13). Of these, the first marks a typical social work approach in which action groups interact with the community not as political activists but as social workers at the micro-level. Often various charitable and philanthropic groups operate with such a welfarist orientation, commonly found in professional social work, as it has developed and been grafted on social science tradition by the state structure controlled by the capitalist ideology. Action groups and voluntary agencies in this stage of development subscribe to the notion of state directed welfarism; they usually adopt an apolitical stance and are disinclined to examine the linkages between a local problem and the nexus of exploitation embedded in broader structures. Hence, at this stage, action groups tend to advocate conformism and mobility within the confines of the system. Their actions are only instrumental in promoting such a mobility. They neither encourage the mobilization of oppressed masses nor do they erode the legitimacy of the state structure in general and the bourgeois capitalist hegemony in particular. Action groups at this welfarist stage believe in moving from top to bottom as the most appropriate strategy of change from within.

In contrast, action groups with a radical nationalist approach generally start building mass movements from the base. In this phase of development, action groups stand for the fundamental democratic rights of the people including the right of self-determination which is perceived as attainable only outside the framework of the existing state structure. Such action groups engage in building alternative structures by mass mobilization no doubt, but do not shake off the bourgeois reformism which they had imbibed consciously or unconsciously (John, 1982: 5-7). Hence, there is no clear-cut break with the capitalist legacy in the case of action groups that are radically-oriented, but anchored in nationalist commitments.

It is in the third stage of development that action groups achieve this breakthrough. Here their radical socialist orientation enables them to develop a vision of an alternative social order, see through the linkages between micro-level conflicts or struggles and the systemic contradictions at the macro-level. Through ideological sharpness, action groups in this stage steer through localized struggles of marginalized sections and work for building alternative mass politics and movements for societal transformation.

Such a neat schema for understanding action groups in terms of stages of their development certainly has a heuristic value but it is based on an assumption of linearity and the transitive character of an action group's stages of development. Empirical realities are, however, far too complex to fit into such a triology of developmental stages in so far as action groups in India are concerned.

For understanding and analyzing action groups, D.L. Sheth (1982) and Harsh Sethi (1984) have developed a classification schema based on considerations (criteria) of the (a) nature of their activities (implying objectives also), and (b) type of organizations behind them (suggesting their ideologies and means). On the basis of the first criterion, Sethi (1984, 306) has classified action groups activities into five categories: (a) relief and charity; (b) development-oriented; (c) mobilization and organization; (d) politics and (e) political education. In terms of organization, however, Sethi puts development and charity groups in one category, and action groups engaged primarily in the processes of conscientization mobilization and organization of the oppressed in another category. Such activist groups are frurther divided into two sub-categories: (a) non-political groups—where a political perspective is either missing or is not stated clearly; and (b) political groups—consisting of those action groups which are formed with explicit political connections or perspectives and goals. All these categories can also be distinguished from pre-party political formations and support-groups. The latter are activist groups formed to carry out the specialized task of bringing out journals, publications or documentation, or lawyer's fora and the like (Sethi, 1984: 306-12). Except the last category of support groups, all the rest in Sethi's scheme had been earlier formulated by Sheth (1982: 7).

There are others, like Dunu Roy, who consider action groups as an expression of the counter ideology operating in any society. Their growth, according to him, takes place through five different stages, namely, charity, development, organization, politics and political education (Roy, 1982). The idea of charity develops into the idea of development which in turn grows into organization, almost similar to an organic evolution. The notion of mass action for development is nothing but a logical short step to 'mass action against those who have so far monopolized the fruits of development' (Roy, 1982). What is surprising in Roy's treatment of the development of action groups is that he views society and social formation as no more than a constant struggle between two world-views opposed to each other. Bordering on crass-idealism, Roy's analysis tends to isolate and separate social phenomena from their material foundations altogether and projects social forces as submitting themselves to omniscient and omnipotent ideas—a position which would be unacceptable to all dialecticians—whether materialist or idealist.

Some activist writers tend to highlight different levels of activities as various phases of the growth process that action groups go through. For example, M.J. Joseph has emphasized the emergence of action groups 'as a result of the efforts consciously made by small groups of concerned people to respond to problems of human misery, exploitation, caste atrocities and similar issues of social injustice.' In this first stage of their development, action groups are spontaneous formations. The second phase corresponds to what might be termed as 'consciousness of the naivete of their earlier unawareness'; in this phase, action groups become gradually conscious of the need to probe into the real forces underlying the problems of poverty, exploitation and atrocities—whether caste, communal, or against women. According to Joseph, the third phase of action groups is marked by their 'search for a broader ideology' (Joseph, 1985: 282-3). Pragmatic concern for political power, application of appropriate strategies and tactics to contain the enemy, and the choice of a political path, all constitute the main elements of the next phase. In the fourth stage, action groups attempt to crystallize a political identity through discussion and exchange of ideas among themselves. Proper machinery for coordination of their activities is then evolved.

Three points emerge clearly from Joseph's approach to the development of action groups: First, their existence is not confined to any particular form or level of activity; rather it is in the process of becoming. Second, this process of becoming is not necessarily initiated by any innate virtue of any level of activity *per se*, but on the contrary it is the result of the contradictions involved at the level of action. Third, therefore, as a result of the contradiction and the action, certain obvious changes are effected in terms of the perception of the situation and organizational efforts on the part of action groups involved (Joseph, 1985).

This line of analysis by Joseph has also been endorsed by Nalini Nayak. According to her, action groups start off more modestly with either straightforward economic or even simple welfare/relief programmes. Those action groups that are sincere and honest in admitting the growing contradictions they encounter while pushing such programmes ahead, are forced to raise questions of propriety and adequacy of their welfare-action, and thus develop their own self-critique. Through such a self-appraisal, action groups discover that there is no other alternative but to launch organizational and organized activity. Such groups, according to Nalini Nayak, may continue to be politically naive for some time but they surely feel the pulse of the people, evoke their participation and involvement in a public cause, and thereby gradually develop the momentum of mass action but outside the national party political stream (Nayak, 1985: 96-99).

Classificatory schema have, of course, their own usefulness in the elementary stages of descriptive and comparative exercises. However, typologies of action groups or of the stages of their development are very often constructed as ideal-types; sometimes they are abstractions based on limited empirical observations. Concrete realities of action groups in India represent a spectrum of a mixture of ideologies, specific goals and means, diverse social background of activists, support bases, organizational activities, and varied linkages with broader political processes and parties. These complexities would undeniably render any general classificatory schema as unacceptable.

Issues of sociological relevance

In assessing the role of action groups in society and in the process of social transformation, it is necessary to turn to more basic and sociologically relevant issues and questions. First, attention must be drawn to the present conditions prevailing in the 'state' and 'civil society,'* i.e., to the structure and institutions and the kind of transformation these are undergoing. An examination of changes taking place in the structural and institutional matrix would reveal as to whether it has outlived its utility, whether or not norms and procedures have lost their meaning and relevance in everyday life, though not their legitimacy, and whether tension, turmoil and unrest resulting from such a situation are building pressures for searching alternative institutions.

Secondly, it is equally important to probe as to whether the model of state-directed development founded on an unstated ideological assumption of mixed capitalist economy blended with the stated choice of a participatory democracy was at all adequate and sound. There is a growing feeling both among masses and among intellectuals that this theory of development and modality of development from top to bottom have not worked, and that there is a growing disenchantment and disillusionment.** Whether in the sphere of work and employment, or food nutrition and health, whether education, housing and environment, or seeds, fertilizers and credit for augmenting productivity in the rural sector, availability and access are visibly restricted. For the masses of rural and urban poor, who constitute an overwhelming majority, the politics of the civil society results only in deprivation and humiliation. Hence, 'new grass-roots level activist groups are engaged in the process of conscientization, searching new alternatives that can in fact work, and realize them through actual struggles' (Kothari,

* The concepts of 'state' and 'civil society' have been used in the sense as in A. Gramsci, 1971: 210-78.

** Such a disenchantment with the policy and practice of rural development has been repeatedly voiced by a number of critics. For example, see Desai, 1983: 3-8; and 1985: 2-4 and 34-38.

1986: 214-15).

What is the relationship between the mainstream politics of the civil society and the new grass-roots politics of masses stirred and awakened by activist groups? Is decline of one necessarily accompanied by the rise of the other? Are these formations party—political and non-party—political processes—antithetical to one another or are they complementary? If they are neither hostile to each other by definition nor instrumental reinforcements, do they run parallel? In that case the co-existence of political processes of the mainstream civil society and the state on the one hand, and non-party mass politics generated by grass-roots level activist groups on the other becomes a central problematic for sociologists aiming at understanding action groups and social transformation in India today.

The role of middle class professionals and intellectuals in verbalizing grievances and issues of marginalized and oppressed is of crucial importance in any study of activist groups. Often it has been stressed that it is the young middle class intellectuals who are increasingly associating themselves with several action groups and micro-level movements that have developed in India in the 1970s onwards to fill the wide political spaces outside the mainstream of party politics and state power (e.g., Sheth, 1982: 3-7). The reasons are not far to seek. Middle class intellectuals, it is generally acknowledged within social science tradition, are endowed with the ability to *declasse* themselves, to transcend their class outlook and to develop a theory—an explanation of any given social reality of which they are themselves a part. With this understanding intellectuals are able to depersonalize struggles, and crystallize ideas into ideologies which propel the process of mobilization of people's movements. Such intellectuals are indispensable for action groups, for they can use ideology to initiate collective action in a structured world. Their articulations involve, what Althusser and Therborn call 'three fundamental modes of ideological interpellations'; namely, they subject and qualify subjects by telling them, relating to them, and making them recognize three things: (a) what exists or does not exist (which includes a prognosis of what has existed before); (b) what is good, right and just as well as its opposites; and (c) what is possible and impossible while patterning or restructuring the world (Therborn, 1982: 18-20). This view is supported by a number of empirical observations about the middle class origins of activist groups in India today.

Kothari, for example, has emphasized that 'in generating the process of mobilization and conscientization and engaging in actual struggles as well as searching for new but workable alternatives, a whole new class of activists has emerged. They are essentially drawn from the conscious and enlightened and troubled streams of the middle class. Some of them engaged themselves in a wide range of activities from the 'Sarvodaya style-constructive work' (in the Gandhian tradition) and non-governmental type development projects to more struggle-oriented political work. It is mostly in the latter type that such middle class intellectuals-turned-activists or animators are able to establish cords with micro-level movements and struggles (Kothari, 1986: 214).

Disenchantment and disillusionment with institutional structures of the state and civil society are almost always highlighted as the reason for middle class urban educated youth and intelligentsia getting drawn into the non-party political formations and processes. A symposium of social activists held recently in New Delhi only reaffirmed the middle class origins of a variety of activist groups in India (Fernandes, 1985). What is interesting to note is the fact that this observation about the predominantly middle class background of activists and action groups holds largely good regardless of whether they are inspired by liberal Sarvodaya type world-view, liberation-theology or by radical-Marxist ideologies.

A number of questions of sociological relevance can again be raised in relation to the role of middle class intellectuals-turned-activists. First, why is there a preponderance of young activists coming from middle class urban backgrounds as compared to those coming from rural subaltern backgrounds? Second, does this mean that middle class activists are more effective in conscientization and mobilization, or are they more successful as verbalizers of ideology, as educators and conscientizers, but not necessarily effective mobilizers? Is it that grass-roots activists, not so articulate in linking micro struggles with macro-level national or international systems of exploitation, like their middle class counterparts, are more effective when it comes to organizing oppressed masses for actual struggles? Similarly, middle class intellectuals-turned-activists often prefer to associate with or involve themselves in non-party political formations and micro-level movements. Why do they seldom take on the task of overhauling the entire state-structure through a reorientation of the mainstream power-politics?

Various alternative explanations of this tendency are possible. The most commonly offered refers to the non-ideological character of power-politics that is flourishing in contemporary polity and the state. Since ideology has little or no function to perform in politics of development, which is really a euphemism for the politics of opportunism, middle class intellectuals generally experience redundancy and tend to withdraw from it. It is also likely that they retreat in acknowledgement of their failure at the macro-level mainstream party-political processes. Or it may be that a kind of romanticism about social transformation and *elan* motivates them to create a micro-level oasis of their own in the form of grass-roots level action groups. The role of an activist releases their creativity, satiates their desire to prove that alternatives to the existing order of things are possible not only in theory but also in practice, and at the same time camouflage their sense of failure, frustration and retreatism with which they had reacted to the broader party-political processes in the civil society. It is also likely that being more sensitive and sensitized to their social responsibilities, urban middle class intellectuals are more conscious of the wide gap that exists between benefits, managed somewhat effortlessly by the middle class professionals, and the plight of the rural and urban poor, as well as of subaltern sections. This awareness further accentuates an excessive sense of guilt among the already sensitized middle-class youth. As an act of expiation then, they turn to grass-roots activism, sometimes by, but often without, renouncing the security anchored in their middle class homes. Such a psycho-analytic explanation of the involvement of middle class youth and intellectuals is also valid logically. However, these questions are basically empirical and would require a series of studies on the social background of activist groups and social movements at the grass-roots level before satisfactory and decisive answers can be obtained.

On a more positive side it could also be argued that action groups' politics give prime importance to the spontaneity of the mass action. The concept of spontaneity denotes that though mass actions are sporadic, unorganized and inarticulate protests, in contrast to organized political struggles of working class, they also have their wisdom and ideology or a world-view of their own (Guha, 1983: 1-7). But then the resurgent masses also search for a new definition of themselves on the one hand and a redefinition of the wider sphere of politics on the other. It is in this process of redefinition that middle class intellectuals turned activists aid the resurgent masses and shape their spontaneity (Kothari, 1984(b): 293) into systematically planned offensives against the system of oppression and exploitation. Linking the micro-level struggles with macro-level processes of transformation, whether political or non-political processes, is another important social function that middle class intellectuals can perform better for the grass-roots level action groups. Thus, 'politics of action-groups can be understood as an attempt to shed the vanguardism of established parties, working-class unions—their leaders and cadres and to demonstrate that the oppressed masses are not just objects of history but can contribute to the transformative process. Action groups, in which middle-class intellectuals involve themselves, thus try to empower the people by reinforcing their actual struggles' (Sheth, 1982; Sethi, 1984: 311-12).

Another important issue that needs attention in relation to the role of intellectuals in action groups is the autonomy of intellectuals vis-a-vis social groups. To frame it differently, the question is whether social groups, including classes and masses, have their own specialized category of intellectuals. The same question has been posited by Gramsci: 'How far are masses and classes able to create one or more strata of organic intellectuals within themselves who give them homogeneity and a sense of awareness of their own function in economic, social and political fields. If they fail to produce their own organic intellectuals, are they able to assimilate any stratum of traditional intellectuals?' (Gramsci, 1971: 5-14). Relating this distinction between the organic and traditional intellectuals, Nalini Nayak has opined that action groups concentrate on action whereas a tiny minority (of intellectuals, mostly university-trained activists from urban areas) goes into broader questions of emerging contradictions in the field and in analyzing them theoretically. What results is an estrangement of intellectual activists from mass-action, and thus organic intellectuals fail to emerge whereas people at the grass-roots are truly starved for creative and theoretical feedback for action (Nayak, 1985: 96-99).

Another important item for sociological inquiry into action groups refers to the way they perceive and analyze present-day crises and contradictions. Some local questions or problems may be understood as non-class contradictions whereas others may be seen as offshoots of class-contradictions, inherent in the system of production as it is assiduously maintained by controllers of economic resources of society and thereby of the state power. If action groups adopt the first approach (non-class contradictions), which is close to the way functionalists approach problems of aberrations or social pathologies, then they would not consider it necessary to go deeper into the roots of what appears to be non-class contradictions or how these developed historically, whether they concern the privations of untouchables (*harijans*), tribals (*adivasis*) or oppression of women and other subaltern sections. If, however, action groups accept the latter view (emphasizing class contradictions) then they would treat socio-cultural contradictions and material contradictions namely those emerging in the process of production as inseparable, expose these contradictions, and understand the historical process of their unfolding as well as the hegemony of the dominant class over the instruments of production and of the state power. Action groups would then evolve a step by step strategy to establish organic links between the struggles at micro-levels and movements at the macro-level for broader social transformation (Kothari, 1984a: 293). Action groups with a radical understanding would undermine the state power as against power of the people, and attempt to turn the mass spontaneity and rhetoric of the people into an instrument of a wider social transformation. However, action groups, approaching problems and crises with a functionalist perspective, would choose to work for consensus, resolve 'non-class' contradictions within the system of existing relations of superordination and subordination, and would not consider it necessary to develop any critical theory of civil society and the state.*

Orthodox Marxism subscribes to a reductionist conception which makes ideology a function of the class position of the subjects. In this epiphenomenal view, social classes by definition have their own paradigmatic ideologies; conversely all ideological elements have a necessary anchor in their class belonging. Action groups and popular movements, in this framework are no more than class-phenomena, or class political actions, only veiled in different forms. Gramsci, however, opposed this economistic conception of ideology and political action. To him the subjects of political action cannot be identified with social classes exclusively; they are in fact collective wills which obey specifically formed laws in view of the fact that they constitute the political expression of hegemonic systems created through ideology. Hence, subjects (i.e., social classes) which exist at the economic level, are not duplicated at the political level. Instead, different inter-class subjects are created (Mouffe, 1979: 188-95). This clearly implies that for Gramsci, hegemony transcends as a simple class alliance; it goes beyond that by creating a superior unity, a fusion of participating elements realized through ideology. While the phenomenon of action groups and people's movements in India could be seen as non-party political processes transcending economistic interests of social classes, the central question is: What kind of ideological unity both

* Some functionalists, like Max Gluckmann and others claim to have incorporated analysis of 'conflict and internal contradictions' within their functionalist paradigm, but, critics of functionalism do not always find this claim to be sufficiently convincing.

within a single group and across different groups, is really reached. This question being empirical in nature, cannot be answered without studies of specific action group formations and popular movements. Nonetheless Gramsci's non-reductionist and more sophisticated conceptions of ideology and political action provide us with a useful framework for such studies.

In this context it would be quite pertinent to refer to Erneste Laclau's theoretical schema to study populism as a possible framework for conceptualizing the phenomena of contemporary action groups and people's movements in India. Moreover, there is a striking influence of Gramsci's approach on Laclau's line of thinking. The analytical framework of Laclau is also based on a non-reductionist conception of politics and ideology. To him classes are 'the poles of antagonistic production relations which have no necessary form of existence at the ideological and political levels' (Laclau, 1977). Following Gramsci, Althusser and Chantal Mouffe, Laclau also endorses a radical critique of pure economism, and points out the twin danger of class reductionism and epiphenomenalism of the economistic perspective of ideology. Both Mouffe and Laclau invoke a kind of an Althusserian alternative principle of over-determination and determination and dominance of a structure versus determination at the last instance by the economic structure (implying production relations). Laclau also asserts that the historical processes at the last instance are determined by relations of production, though temporarily they may be dominated by religious, political and cultural (non-economic) ideas and institutions. In short, according to Laclau, the existence of classes at the ideological and political levels can no longer be explained in a reductionist economistic frame of reference. This means that classes exist at the ideological and political level in the process of articulation of their constituent interpellations and not in the process of reduction. More importantly, articulation requires the existence of non-class contents—interpellations and contradictions—which constitute the raw materials on which class ideological practices dominate. Finally, Laclau also conclusively suggests that classes and empirically observable groups do not necessarily coincide (Laclau, 1977: 159-63). To him, people/power bloc contradiction is the dominant contradiction at the level of the social formation if class contradiction is dominant at the level of the mode of production. People is then not just a rhetorical concept but constitutes one of the two poles of contradictions, at the level of concrete social formation whose intelligibility depends on the *ensemble* of political and ideological relations of domination and not just the relations of production (Laclau, 1977: 107-8). Yet still, Laclau, like Althusser, subscribes to the general principle of over-determination and determination at the last instance by economic class ideologies and contradictions. This framework has tremendous potentialities which can be used fruitfully for comparing and explaining action groups operating at different levels, with equally diverse goals, means, organizational links and ideological outlook in contemporary India. This paper makes a strong plea for further explorations in Laclau's analytical schema and in examining its relevance to the understanding of action groups and people's movement phenomena in India.

Methodology of intervention and participatory research that most activist groups follow also call for some attention, Some activists assert that action groups have been successful, though in a limited way, in developing an adequate methodology of working with the people which leads to an emergence of an autonomous, strong and lasting movement (Volken, 1985: 14). Those who adopt a conventional social work approach favour the strategy of working for the people more than working with the people; they do not necessarily accept methods of intervention and participation. The former methodology has been widely used by action groups, particularly by professional charity or philanthropic organizations, as well as by governmental and non-governmental development agencies in India.

Advocacy in favour of participatory methods is often based on the assumption that unity of the subject and object of study deepens understanding and provides an insider's view that an outsider's so called objective inquiry seldom develops. Without such insights or reflexivity an activist would not develop a critical understanding (or a theory of the problem he is handling which alone can guide remedial action) nor would action groups be able to mobilize people effectively.*

Some activists have complained that the prolonged presence of action groups at the grass-roots level tends to develop a sense of dependency among the people. In fact people's consciousness grows by exercizing responsibility and self-decision making or action. However, activists sometimes become subtle mechanisms of control and inhibit growth of self-consciousness among the people (Volken, 1985: 27-28). Hence, the activist role should essentially remain that of an outsider; action groups should work as mobile teams stimulating analytical thinking and helping people as well as participants of such action groups to place facts and events in their socio-economic, political and cultural perspective. The question really is whether with outsider identity, action groups can develop reflexivity in their understanding—a precondition for launching effective struggles and mass movements.

For sociologists, the main issue is what potentialities participatory method or the method of sociological intervention has in understanding social reality and whether micro-level involvement of sociologists with action groups would yield them a highly localized understanding which has limited use in analyzing or explaining broader social processes at the macro-level. What kind of social theory one develops through intervention and whether it would advance 'scientific' theory of society as such?

Social intervention and participatory methods raise the broader issues of science, scientific method, its objectivity and valuefreeness—of more general issues in the philosophy of science which cannot possibly be dealt with within the ambit of this study. However, it is important to recognize that there exist two distinct viewpoints on the desirability of social intervention on the part of the analyst: (a) The purists in social nces always emphasize the dichotomy between analyst and catalyst. The former simply

* For a detailed discussion on the concept of reflexivity in sociology, or 'reflexive sociology', see Gouldner, 1970: 488-504.

produces a theoretical understanding and maintains value-neutrality or complete detachment, whereas the latter uses that theoretical knowledge for making intervention in a social situation more meaningful and purposeful. (b) There are others who believe that this is a misplaced dichotomy and cannot be valid at all. To them analysis and praxis are as inseparable as two sides of the same coin, because a theoretical analysis realizes itself in the action dictated by it and the latter seeks legitimacy in the former. While we tend to side with the second viewpoint, it is necessary to stress that social analysts must assert some measure of autonomy, but not self-righteousness, some distance but not isolation vis-a-vis catalysts or activists. At least such an autonomy would help the analyst in demystifying intervention whenever it is pushed too far and becomes an end in itself and when it tantamounts to imposition of the activists' consciousness on the spontaneity of the people's movement.

Sustenance dilemma: foreign funds and action groups

All activist groups—large or small—tend to develop an organizational structure of their own. Sustenance of these organizations, through full-time activists working at the grass-roots level, requires funds and other material resources. It is common knowledge that in many developing countries, action groups have been receiving funds through foreign agencies based in the developed western capitalist countries. One of the polemical issues concerning action groups in India today, therefore, concerns the use of foreign funds.

The number of funding agencies in the developed world has multiplied over the years. Foreign aid has, therefore, played a significant role in the growth of NGOs and action groups. Sometimes funds are channelled through official/state controlled agencies, but philanthropic and voluntary organizations, including private trusts are also not lagging behind in providing funds to support developmental or ameliorative activity in the less developed countries. Growing privatization of aid can be at least partly explained in terms of the tax-exemption granted by government as a financial incentive for promoting the voluntary sector.

For example, in the area of health, environment, population control, education, religion and relief for the poor and distressed, many private entrepreneurs and business houses as well as voluntary organizations in the United States are coming forward to help because of tax-exemptions. Such an aid, when offered within the domestic setting, definitely reduces the pressure on the welfare state. Sometimes donors also prefer private funds because of their disillusionment with the institutions of government (Pifer, 1987: 123-29). When such an aid is offered internationally, it is often purported to create bilateral goodwill.

Problems arise when this philanthrophy is extended beyond nation-states' boundaries. Moreover, some of the aid agencies no longer operate purely with the old-fashioned philanthropic or charity orientation. They believe that 'voluntary aid ought to try and stimulate social action, shape public opinion, monitor governments (particularly in the Third World) and to influence, through lobbying, 'the development of public policies to affect social change' (Pifer, 1987:130). It is only when foreign aid has diplomatic strings attached to it that its acceptance raises moral issues and the question of propriety. Whether or not the donors' motives and ideological orientations adhere with those of the recipient action groups in the developing world is the central question that has been debated rather hotly in the activist circles in more recent years.

Many radical scholars are now becoming increasingly apprehensive of the devastating clout foreign aid still holds in the activities of NGOs and voluntary action groups, particularly in India. For example, Prakash Karat has castigated action groups in India characterizing them as essentially disruptive and as integral parts of the imperialist strategy of penetration of post-colonial societies. Such voluntary groups are proliferated, through foreign funds, primarily to influence the course of development of the respective societies in which they operate. Karat even suspects that the NGOs, voluntary action groups and mass movements are systematically used by the forces of imperialism to counter and weaken the potential of the Left movement in India (Karat, 1984: 19-54;

1985: 812). He does not spare even the international agencies such as the International Monetary Fund (IMF), World Bank, Populational Council and the like. This viewpoint has been countered fervently by Harsh Sethi who has defended action groups receiving foreign funds. To him aid *per se* is not objectionable; terms and conditions of funding can be. When the subaltern classes hardly have enough to survive, much less to support others, there is nothing wrong if funds are secured from outside the class (Sethi, 1985: 378-79). When governments do not hesitate to receive foreign aid to promote their own developmental programmes why should NGOs and action groups hold back their hands moralistically, if donors offer funds voluntarily? This line of argument is at best pragmatic but it bypasses the broader questions of morality, integrity and commitment of the activists. The compatibility of the donor's motives and ideological objectives with those of the recipient action groups is a vital consideration and can be ignored only to the detriment of the cause action groups work for.

Recognizing the fact that practical problems of organization of action groups cannot simply be wished away, Ajit Roy also finds nothing objectionable, in principle, in groups accepting foreign funds, but suggests that such decisions ought to be taken with discretion and on the merits of each specific case of foreign agency offering funds. Some of them may have sinister aims but there are others who are genuinely progressive in their outlook and would like to promote any transformative action group. Roy goes to the extent of saying that there is 'nothing wrong in using funds coming from reactionary sources for progressive causes'. All that the action groups have to ensure is that such funds are not used clandestinely to curb their own radical activities, that they do not develop total dependency on these sources of funding, and finally, that easy flow of foreign money would not have a corrupting influence on their own activists (Roy, 1985: 133).

Wishful thinking about what foreign aid ought or ought not to do to action groups is no remedy for the hard reality of what it actually does. H. Volken argues that for most of the action groups in India, the main thrust of people's movement at the grass-roots has shifted from liberation to development. Full-time animators of action groups, with economistic goals, constantly require financial assistance and infrastructures to launch self-sustaining developmental activities. Foreign funding agencies are also keen to promote those programmes of conscientization which yield quick results in bringing benefits in housing, health, rural employment, literacy or any income-generating or supplementing activities. This, Volken thinks, makes development more visible rather than the distant dream of socialist ideology. But he admits that the craze of action groups for foreign funds, though, may have led to accumulation of assets for groups and a comfortable living for their full-time activists, often plays a decisive role in breaking up of such groups. On a more positive side, foreign funds enable action groups to replicate the people's movement in another area, organize training camps, and support-structures without losing their credibility (Volken, 1985: 20-22). What is rather surprising is that Volken's optimism almost borders on a pious hope that foreign assistance does not necessarily restrict the freedom of action groups.

On the issue of foreign funds, Rajesh Tandon and Ganesh Pandey (Fernandes ed., 1985: 103-9) have taken a bold, but in quintessence, a pragmatic stand. They have deprecated the tendency of treating action groups accepting foreign funds as 'untouchables' when the government and political parties negotiate and freely accept foreign aid, and academic institutions are hailed when they secure foreign funds for their research programmes while industrial/business houses are given incentives to enter into foreign collaboration to modernize their technologies. While all forms of hypocrisy, double standards and 'holier-than-thou' attitude must be despised, it is difficult to accept the indispensability and desirability of foreign funds for action groups as Tandon and Pandey do.

Interestingly enough activists of all ideological shades engaged in different kinds of conscientization programmes—whether liberation or development-oriented—justify acceptance of foreign funds almost uncritically, and simply reiterated that action groups must neither develop dependency on foreign assistance nor succumb to external pressures from donors. But it is indeed difficult to adhere to both these factors simultaneously. International aid agencies and their networks of patronage have penetrated so deep into developing countries that their pressures are seldom explicit; these are exercised too subtly for the micro-level groups in action to realize initially. When they do realize that they are being constrained, it is already too late. We believe that parasitism in any form cannot be advocated for building a genuine people's movement. A real people's movement has to be fully indigenous and self-reliant. How to sustain the activists, animators and their support-structures over a long period of time is a challenge, that is an integral part of the tasks of action groups, and not to be consigned to foreign agencies to meet.

Action groups aspiring to provide a non-party political alternative in India must not seek legitimacy from either governmental or foreign agencies, from political parties, trade unions or from academics, nor should they insulate themselves from all these either. Getting locked into cocoons of micro-level activity can of course provide a sense of fulfilment and achievement on a limited scale but it can also turn the programme of broader macro-level transformation into a romanticized dream like 'the Holy Grail'. To encourage a constant dialogue among action groups on goals, both distant and proximate, on perspectives and methodology, interaction with support structures is required. A completely open-door policy would undoubtedly lead to confusion and blurred identity, but a total insulation could be equally self-defeating. Only a careful blend of ideological commitment and pragmatism, macro-perspective and micro-level involvements, discourse with outsiders, but awareness of self- autonomy, and discretion in accepting both allies and financial help would alone unfold the inherent strength of action groups, if they are to become a viable as well as a stable alternative in the social transformation process in India.

References

Desai, A.R. 1983, *A New Policy for Rural Development in South and South-East Asia: Its Sinister Significance.* Bombay: C.G. Shah Memorial Trust (Publication No. 19).

1985. *Changing Profile of Rural Society in India.* Bombay: C.G. Shah Memorial Trust (Publication No. 7).

Dhanagare, D.N. 1983. *Peasant Movements in India, 1920-1950.* Delhi: Oxford University Press.

1984 'Agrarian Reform and Rural Development in India: Some Observations', *Research in Social Movements, Conflict and Change,* Vol. 7.

Fernandes, W. (Ed.). 1985. *Social Activists and People's Movements.* New Delhi: Indian Social Institute.

Gouldner, A.W. 1970. *The Coming Crisis in Western Sociology.* New York: Basic Books.

Gramsci, A. 1971. *Selections from the Prison Notebooks.* London: Lawrence and Wishart.

Guha, R. (Ed.). 1982. *Subaltern Studies,* Vol. I, Delhi: Oxford University Press.

1983. *Elementary Aspects of Peasant Insurgency in Colonial India.* Delhi: Oxford University Press.

John, J. 1982. 'Critique of Action Groups', *The Marxist Review* (August issue)—reproduced by the Resource Centre for People's Education and Development, Madurai.

Joseph, M.J. 1985. 'Action Groups in India and their Challenges to the Institutional Churches', *Jeevadhara—A Journal of Christian Interpretation,* Vol. XV, No. 88 (July 1985) Special Number on 'Church as People's Movement'.

Karat, P. 1984. 'Action Groups/Voluntary Organizations: A Factor in Imperialist Strategy', *The Marxist,* Vol. 2, April-June.

1985. 'Justification for Imperialist-Financed Activities', *Economic and Political Weekly,* Vol. XX, No. 18, 4 May.

Kothari, R. 1984a. 'Grass-roots', *Seminar* (January).

1984b. 'The Non-Party Political Process', *Economic and Political Weekly,* Vol. XX, No. 5, February 4.

1986. 'Masses, Classes and the State'. *Economic and Political Weekly,* Vol. XXI, No. 5, 1 February.

Laclau, E. 1977. *Politics and Ideology in Marxist Theory,* London: Verso Edition.

Mouffe, C. (Ed.). 1979. *Gramsci and Marxist Theory.* London: Routledge and Kegan Paul.

Nayak, N. 1985. 'Where are the Action Groups Today?' in W. Fernandes (Ed.) 1985, *op. cit.*

Pifer, A. 1987. 'Philanthropy, Voluntarism and Changing Times', *Daedalus,* Winter 1987.

Roy, A. 1985. 'Activist Groups-Fundamental Issues' in W. Fernandes (Ed.), 1985, *op. cit.*

Roy, D. 1982, *Between Dogma and Debate*—'The Problem of Communication between Groups and Individuals Engaged in Social Development and Change,' Bombay: BUILD-Documentation Centre (Background Paper No. 5).

Sethi, H. 1984. 'Groups in a New Politics of Transformation,' *Economic and Political Weekly,* Vol. XIX, No. 7, 18 February.

1985. 'The Immoral Other: The Debate between Party and Non-party Groups', *Economic and Political Weekly,* Vol. XX, No. 9, 2 March.

Sheth, D.L. 1982. 'Movements,' *Seminar,* No. 278, October.

1984. 'Grass-roots Initiatives in India', *Economic and Political Weekly,* Vol. XIX, No. 6, 11 February.

Therborn, G. 1982. *The Ideology of Power and the Power of Ideology.* London: Verso Editions.

Touraine, A. 1981. *The Voice and the Eye-Study of Social Movements,* Cambridge University Press and Paris-Maison des Sciences de L' Hommes.

Volken, H. 1985. 'Action Groups: Beginning or End of a Dream', in W. Fernandes (Ed.), 1985, *op. cit.*

Chapter eight

Relevance of sociology: some determinants

The discipline of sociology has gained considerable respectability and acceptability in the eyes of public at large as much as in the estimation of their fellow social scientists since the Second World War. Despite this growing recognition, sociology has also become an omnibus science—highly diversified in its subject-matter and analytical perspectives and equally, or even more, complex in its methodologies and applications. In terms of conceptual categories or theoretical approaches it has become increasingly difficult to claim sociology to be a unified body of knowledge any longer. Within the professional circles of sociologists themselves, perceptions or images of the discipline differ widely.

Broadly these images of sociology[1] could be classified into five categories: (a) The positivist image of sociology treats sociology as a pure science that aims at a value-free, objective causal analysis and at offering scientific explanation of social phenomena. Within such a positivist frame of reference a science often claims to have developed capacity to generate general laws and make predictions. (b) The view of sociology as fundamentally a part of 'humanities' is quite in divergence with the first image. Here the thrust is on 'understanding' through reflexivity the humanist ethos and cultural creativity of all forms of social existance rather than on predictions. In this image, 'sociological perspective is a broad, open and an emancipated vista on human life and a sociologist is inwardly open to the measureless richness of human possibilities, eager for new horizons and new worlds of meaning'. Such an image of sociology comes close to what **Peter Berger** (1963: 25-53) calls 'sociology as a form of consciousness'. (c) The third image of sociology is that it constitutes a set of rules, just like a grammar, which facilitates communication through shared symbolic structures. In this somewhat hermeneutic concept of sociology, its function is similar to that of a language of discourse. (d) The most common perception of sociology is that it is 'social engineering', and that its task is basically 'applied', rather than 'purely analytical'. In this interventionist conception of sociology, the discipline is treated as a problem solving craft. (e) Finally, at least some hold 'sociology', or for that matter every social science discipline, as basically a 'world-view', an ideology which either tacitly or explicitly states the desired end-states to which processes of social transformation ought to move and which broadly indicate the lines of inquiry as well as methodological options open to a sociologist within a given socio-cultural matrix.

Although these categories are analytically separable, in reality professional sociologists' images of their craft often manifest in curious combinations. The issue of relevant sociology or relevance of sociology is therefore likely to be settled quite differently depending on what images practitioners of sociology have in their minds.

In any discussion on 'relevance' of a social science discipline one cannot possibly have pretensions of being totally value-free. No matter whether relevance is being examined from the standpoint of a practitioner of a craft, from the prespective of the professional community the practitioner belongs to, or whether it is being assessed in terms of the expectations society at large has from the practitioner, value-loads are built-in in any such assessment. For that matter they are inescapable in any evaluative exercise which is basically normative.

It is an interesting question in the sociology of knowledge as to why the issue of relevance of social sciences, including sociology, is being raised and debated frequently in the 1980s. Both from within the analyst's psyche and from outside the question of relevance has been raised in more recent years. Two points are particularly noteworthy here: (i) Such a discussion is a reflection on the growing self-awareness of sociologists, their willingness to question the very foundations of sociology and also on their keenness to assess the epistemological assumptions underlying sociological theories and concepts as well as ontology of the nature of man and consciousness. (ii) Secondly, significantly enough, those who are *not* in power are not asking the question of relevance of sociology. But those in power often raise it. Hence, when professional sociologists discuss the issue of relevance it is likely to be interpreted either as an act of self-defence or as an expression of powerlessness in the wider arena of socio-political system.

Freedom versus social conditioning

The most pertinent question, however, is who decides what is 'relevant sociology' and 'what is the relevance of sociology'? Both the questions, though framed differently, are in quintessence quite similar. No single answer to such questions would evoke agreement. It could be argued that sociology investigates all dimensions of social reality and in using its theories and methods the discipline as well as its practitioners must have intellectual freedom, implying freedom from all constraints—political or ideological. If the logic of this argument is followed seriously, then 'relevance' becomes an exclusive realm of scientists themselves—in this case of professional sociologists. An alternative, and an equally cogent, argument could be that sociology and sociologists free from all constraints and contexts, can be anything but realistic. The entire discipline of sociology emerged as a response to challenges posed by the growth of industrial capitalism in the West. The cultural and social context, in which knowledge production takes place, conditions and shapes that production process considerably. Hence, 'there are closer contextual and existential linkages between dominant paradigms and socio-historical forces at a given time' (Singh, 1984-5). Relevance of sociology in this alternative frame is determined by the conditions or context in which it is debated and decided.

'Intellectual autonomy of sociology' is thus pitted against social conditioning (even determination) of knowledge. Both these formulations are polar-type abstractions, typifications and, to a certain extent, ideological mystifications that tend to miss the dialectical connections between the two. Moreover, internal coherence of these two 'ideal-type' positions is more often taken for granted than it is subjected to critical discussions.

Freedom of sociologists in deciding what is 'relevant sociology' at a given time and place itself is more of a 'desired end-state' rather than a reality. Since we assume that 'fact' and 'value' are inseparable in any understanding or reconstruction of social reality, freedom and autonomy of sociologist is as much a reality as it is a value-judgement and value-assertion. Such a mixture of fact and value is true even in the case of social conditioning of knowledge. One needs to recall only the major theoretical and methodological orientations that dominated thought and action of scientists in the nineteenth century. Positivism, rationalism, utilitarianism, existentialism and dialectical materialism could be mentioned as some of the dominant paradigms during the age of early industrialism and its sustenance through the colonial system. The science of society—sociology—developed as a separate discipline not because it had readymade theoretical paradigms to fall back upon but largely because its practitioners were able to synthesize these. Such syntheses were partly dictated and necessitated by social conditions in which they were attempted by classical thinkers and were partly outcomes of individual analysts' special or unique ways of understanding as well as of their intellectual sensitivities. The positivist paradigm exemplifies this kind of synthesis.

Methodologies and relevance

Positivism is a case in point particularly because Comte had launched sociology on the foundations of what he called as the new system of positive philosophy. It in a sense has a built-in criterion of defining what is relevant and what is not relevant for a sociologist committed to positivism. As a general approach in sociology, positivism emphasized the identity between the social and the natural or physical sciences, stressed on direct observation or proof as the only valid and ultimate source of knowledge (i.e., a definite epistemology) and aimed at formulation of general laws. In the

Galilean-Newtonean tradition positivism asserted 'formulation of general laws and prediction' as the ultimate goal of every scientific endeavour.

The classical sociologists Marx, Spencer, Weber and Durkheim were all influenced by positivism which constituted the intellectual foundation of their age. Yet, each one of them responded to the social and economic changes of their time as he understood the relevance of his enterprise. Instead of getting captivated by existing paradigms, they not only used them but also modified or amended them with creative and innovative zeal. Thus, organicists, holists, emergentist-functionalists considered themselves no less positivist than methodological individualists. Similarly, 'Marxists attempted to unite empiricist scientific tradition with historicism on the one hand and anti-analytical holism on the other' (Saran, 1962: 200). In other words, the classical thinkers in the sociological tradition adhered to a given paradigm to a certain extent and defined its relevance in the context of socio-historical forces of their times although the latter sometimes required them to tread a different path.

Weber's commitment to positivism had different shades. Under the intellectual impact of Wilhelm Dilthey, who was avowedly a non-positivist, it is unlikely that Weber did not inherit some scepticism of his mentor towards doctrinaire positivism. Nonetheless, he considered only that sociology as relevant and scientific which conforms to canons of objectivity and value-neutrality (Freund, 1972: 37-86). In this way, on the one hand Weber shared Marxists' commitment to 'empiricist-scientific tradition' in methodological terms, but on the other hand he challenged the latter's materialistic reductionism as unacceptable. Weber's search for an alternative to the materialist paradigm landed him on idealistic reassertions, best exemplified in his thesis on 'Protestant ethic and the spirit of capitalism'. Another important departure from the hard core nineteenth century positivism is to be found in Weber's notion of sociology as an interpretative science. To him 'exegesis' and understanding, and not prediction, was the ultimate goal of social inquiry. He did not share the Marxist view that unity of science via a single set of laws is possible. Rather, Weber thought that although the study of society has to be objective and scientific, its laws are held to be unique unlike those of physics and other terrestrial sciences. The relevance of what sociology does must not therefore be decided by the yardsticks of physical sciences.

In short, though positivism was inescapable in their times, all classical sociologists defined its relevance and contextualized it in accordance with priorities perceived by them and in response to the socio-historical forces they confronted. Partly the relevance of a paradigm was a given matter for them, but partly they exercised their autonomy and freedom and through critical reflection made innovations creatively in setting its scope and limits in studying social reality as they thought it was relevant.

An important debate in the philosophy of science refers to 'explanation' versus 'prediction' as appropriate model for social science inquiry or for behavioural research. One group of methodologists argues that a good explanation is one which has ability to predict. Carl Hempel and P. Oppenheim, for example, take the position that if an explanation does not allow predictions, then it is not adequate. In their view explanation and prediction are two bits of knowledge which stand in a certain logical relation to one another, and parts of the same deductive systematization (Hempel *et al.*, 1948: 135-75). In recent years, however, methodologists and philosophers of science have increasingly emphasized the difference between explanation and prediction. The former is about an actuality implying that a counter-factuality can prove it to be wrong, while there is no corresponding actuality for an unsuccessful prediction. Kaplan is of the view that explanations provide 'understanding' and may be able to suggest future trends that are not necessarily predictions. Hence, we can predict without being able to understand, and can understand reality without necessarily being able to predict (Kaplan, 1964: 349-51).

The question of relevance of sociology too cannot be considered in isolation from this important methodological debate. Those who consider 'prediction' as the ultimate test of science would tend to apply the rigorous criteria of relevance drawn from the models of natural sciences. In spite of the growing realization even among natural scientists that even this hard-core positivism has serious limitations, protagonists of such a view find in it a useful stick to beat behavioural sciences with and to tame them into accepting a subordinate role vis-a-vis natural scientists. Frequently, national developmental priorities and fundings are decided on the basis of usefulness of a science. This 'usefulness' is judged by their ability to identify cause by controlling other variables and then to 'predict'. All the rest, including social sciences, are considered not so 'relevant' since they are regarded as lacking the ability to attempt causal analyses and make predictions with precision and accuracy. Social sciences are then left with the only option of either competing with each other to prove their 'degree of usefulness', or alternatively to be content with redundancy more often thrust on them by their counterparts in natural sciences who prove themselves to be more successful and enterprising salesmen in the eyes of powers that be. There are others who believe that even without acquiring the 'so-called predictive ability', understanding is a legitimate scientific task which is no less socially relevant.

The domination of empirical scientific sociology continued to be felt until recently. This brand of sociology, consciously or unconsciously, subscribed to a particular epistemological view and to an objective approach to social reality. Sociologists, in this tradition, sincerely believed that complete objectivity is not only desirable but also possible and that it constitutes the best route to build scientific understanding. Sociologists with this act of faith confined themselves to an outsider's role and seldom attempted to develop capacity to empathize with the subjective consciousness of the people whom they studied. A sociologist is now being expected increasingly to combine the objectivity of the outsider and the 'reflexivity' of the insider. It is the blend of the two called reflexive sociology—which sets the standards of relevance[2]. 'Reflexivity implies capacity to develop a disciplined mind, conceptual clarity, a dialectical universe of discourse and commitment to values of humanity and universality' (Singh, 1984b: 7). This capacity cannot simply grow until sociologists remain obsessed both with ultra-positivist tenets of 'predictability' and with 'value-freeness' that prevent any sharing of symbolic cultural meanings and communication between the observer and the observed.

Sociological theory and the question of relevance

The theoretical paradigms play a significant role in the development of any science. A theory offers a general explanation of social reality and hence it is a higher level abstraction than general laws. In fact laws serve to explain empirical events, which are time and place specific, whereas theories explain laws (Kaplan, 1964: 346-47). Regardless of whether our interest is in scientific reconstruction for making 'prediction' or whether it is confined to only 'understanding', theoretical constructs are indispensable for any effort that claims to be a scientific activity. The record of sociology in developing theoretical paradigms has not been any less impressive than that of any other social science discipline. These constructions range from metatheories and grand-theories to middle range ones. Marxism (historical materialism as a theory), functionalism (both in its organicist and in structuralist-cultural ramifications), systems theory, structuralism and phenomenology at one end and symbolic interactionism, exchange theory, ethnomethodology, reference-group and the like at the other end constitute the broad spectrum of sociological theories.

In a scientific community theoretical approaches lay down the ground rules for discourse both at the institutional and intellectual levels. Each of these approaches spells out its analytical schema, conceptual apparatus and methodological priorities. As internally coherent systems of thought theoretical constructs are supposed to be fountain-heads of new ideas, new models and insights and of originality and creativity. However, once formulated theories soon begin to serve as a source of identity among adherents of a particular theory. They tend to treat their theory as a water-tight compartment, more as a finished product than as a process of enrichment of knowledge and understanding, more as a dogma than as a set of deductively interrelated set of propositions, and more as a sectional possession rather than a common asset to be shared by the entire scientific community. Theories then become dysfunctional to truly scientific endeavour as they raise structural barriers to a genuinely intellectual discourse and to creativity. The structure of intellectual life, particularly when it is institutionalized, inevitably builds into it an element of conflict, which paradoxically is non-intellectual, and even anti-intellectual in nature. Theoretical schools then tend to become fortifications from where offensives are launched to undermine claims to relevance made by rival schools or positions. Theories then become stagnant and dogmatic restatements. The fragementary view of theoretical constructs or paradigms is thus largely dictated by non-intellectual pressures and considerations of careers and positions in a scientific community. Practising sociologists under such an intellectual climate to some extent become prisoners of their education. Unfortunately, the scientific vision of sociology has been blurred by such pressures which can be attributed to the rapid quantitative expansion of sociology. This is how Randall Collins (1986: 1336-38) characterizes the real crisis of sociology in the 1980s.

Raising the boundary-walls between supposedly distinct theories was detrimental to the synthetic ethos of sociology which had demonstrated its capacity to harmonize and integrate formal with concrete, logical with phenomenological and transcendent with the historical realms of reality (Singh, 1984a: 1-2). Since fortunately practising sociologists, both in the developed as well as developing countries, found their relevance only in being responsive to the historically and culturally specific social processes, changes in the theoretical paradigms were inevitable. Through their adoption in application, operationalization, testing and in reconstructions, theories passed through stages of refinement and modification as also through synthesis.

In the 1970s and 1980s, therefore, the unnatural boundaries between theories have started crumbling down. In formulating research questions as well as in analyzing and interpreting their data, most of the practising sociologists in the developed as well as in the developing countries have discovered points of convergence and, what Yogendra Singh calls of 'paradigmatic convolusion' (Singh, 1984a, 1984b). This trend was set by the development of critical theory school or the works of the Frankfurt school which attempted to show the humanist ethos of Marx's theory of alienation which is rooted in certain Hegelian notions. Some of the school members tried to unite psychoanalysis and Marxism—an effort which was bound to evoke a sharp reaction from orthodox Marxists. From Adorno to Hebarmas this spirit of synthesis and innovation with paradigms has dominated the growth of critical theory (Bottomore, 1984). On the other side we find Althusserian attempt to construct structuralist Marxism. Drawing heavily on Levi-Strauss' categories of formal relations such as homology, symmetry, inversion, opposition and binary division, Althusser tries to redefine the Marxist notion of totality in pure structuralist terms, where unit of analysis is 'structure' rather than individual. His approach to Marxism is both anti-historicist and anti-humanistic (Rex, 1974) as it treats structural analysis of the existing contradictions as more relevant than historical materialism as such.

Such attempts towards theoretical synthesis are unabated even today and are pointers of the multi-dimensionality of social reality on the one hand and the limitations of the universalistic claims made by protagonists of specific theoretical paradigms on the other. This is not to suggest that pursuit of theorization and theoretical abstraction is a futile exercise. Rather, the discussion simply aims at pointing out how rigid, though rigorous, adoption of a theoretical approach does not necessarily render one study or analytical exercise more relevant than the other. It only shows that all theoretic approaches and paradigms are relevant; depending on what problem one is studying, and how complex is the reality being approached, a certain theoretic construct, or a specific blend of two or more of them, may turn out to be more relevant than the other. No theoretical approach by definition can, therefore, be dismissed as either untenable logically or irrelevant empirically.

Ideology and relevance

The affinity between theory and ideology renders the question of 'relevance of sociology' a praxeological one. Ideology refers to a set of beliefs and ideas about facts, causal relations and values in human affairs which reinforce one another either through logic or through affinity of sentiments inspired by them, and at least some of which are unverified or unverifiable. As a set of ideas and beliefs ideology seeks (a) to articulate the basic values of a group of people, and (b) to distribute power-in-society. Ideology in itself is neither philosophy nor a systematic theory (Apter, 1964: 15-46). Values denote the abstract side of ideology but it is less abstract than philosophy; power is the other dimension of ideology since ideology realizes itself through concrete actions towards the attainment of power without which it is difficult to draw oneself closer to the desired end-states. As a guide to these actions ideologues draw heavily on social theory and analysis.

The problem of the relation of ideologies to scientific analysis and theories is posited more directly in Marxism. In his *Theses on Feurbach*, Marx had stressed:

> The philosophers have only interpreted the world in various ways; the point however is to change it (as cited in Lukacs, 1971).

Theory and praxis thus form integral parts of the Marxist world-view. It is the unity of the two which is stressed in orthodox Marxist social thought. The central problem in Marxism is not of how one understands, analyzes and theorizes, but how to use that theoretical understanding or analysis for praxis—for changing reality in the directions set ideologically.

Marxist sociology, therefore, lays down the ground rules of 'relevance'. In his *Critique of Hegel's Philosophy of Right*, Marx clearly states the conditions in which a relation between theory and practice becomes possible. 'It is not enough that thought should seek to realize itself, reality must also strive towards thought. It is only when consciousness stands in relation to reality can theory and practice (thought and action) be united. For this to happen emergence of consciousness must become the decisive step. The historical function of theory is to make this step a practical possibility' (Marx, 1970 ; also G. Lukacs, 1971).

Orthodox Marxism, however, takes a rather dogmatic and rigid view of the theory-action relationship as inseparable; any theory which has no potentiality to assume the form of an ideology-suggesting the lines or directions of social and political activism is treated as irrelevant. More liberal Marxists, however, consider studied criticism and analysis as a legitimate way of building a science. One of the important functions of sociology is to offer 'social criticism' which aims at demystification of the ruling class ideology (Bottomore, 1974: 90-94) because mystification is the principal source of alienation. The task of social criticism is to unmask the disguised forms alienation takes, whether in the realm of religion, power-politics or in the process of production. In the 1950s the Frankfurt School took up precisely this task of building 'critical theory' or 'critical sociology'. Its contention was that criticism is an equally relevant method of building a science because (a) it helps to clarify one's own notions; (b) through social criticism sociologist can effectively conscientize others; through critical analysis social scientist can expose the elements of mystification in any theory/ideology; and (c) thereby an analyst, through criticism can contribute significantly to social action and change (Singh, 1984b: 12).

The praxeological thrust and ideological overtones in Marxism are self-evident. These have tended to be more implicit or even veiled in functionalism and in systems theory of the Parsonian variety. Here the problem of social order is viewed within a moralistic frame, with explicit fascination for conservatism. The dual commitment in Parsons to positivism and functionalism has the third dimension, i.e., obsession with *status quo* and resistance to change (Gouldner, 1970: 251-54). Postulates of these theories are based on assumptions about role, status, institutions and normative structures. Above all premises regarding functional integration or capacities of structures or systems to restore their equilibrium sound more like ideological assertions rather than factual statements. Problems of conflict and change were not ignored by functionalists and Parsons' systems paradigm altogether but then 'conflict' came to be treated as dysfunctional, and change, as an end product of 'structural differentiation' which takes place only within the boundary-maintaining system that has inherent capacity for re-equilibrium and homeostasis (Parsons, 1970: 480-503). In American sociology these orientations determined its own relevance and influenced considerably the choices of both methods and themes of study. From family and marriage to criminality/deviance, and from group dynamics in large scale formal organizations, including labour-management relations to problems of integration and assimilation of ethnic or immigrant groups, constituted some of the research themes in American sociology from the 1930s to 1950s and 1960s or so. The conceptual categories used frequently in these studies pertained to deviation or conformity, adjustment or adaptation or stability, order, solidarity and integration, which resulted in the mystification of theory of role, status and structure. Empirical findings of studies with functionalist and systems theoretical orientation were suggestive of coping strategies for problems encountered in interpersonal relations whether in families, ethnic neighbourhoods, hospitals, army establishments, prisons or in large scale industrial organizations[3]. In short 'applied' sociology became more relevant as it served the needs of the ruling classes in the United States. This brand of sociology was susceptible to the influence of establishment ideology and it was exposed by C.Wright Mills (1962: 525-52) as early as in 1943.

The critical sociology tradition, however, gathered momentum once again in western sociology only in the 1960s when the massive student protests on university campuses in the wake of the American involvement in the Vietnam War had unleashed new historical forces. These protests developed into radical social movements throughout North America including Canada (Bottomore, 1969: 80-118). It is worth noting that 'crisis' in western sociology came to be discussed only in the context of such developments that questioned not only adequacy but also propriety of certain theoretical orientations (Gouldner, 1970). But then this crisis was visible in Marxism and Marxist sociology as well. Ideological dogmatism beneath orthodox Marxism came under attack not only from within the Frankfurt School but also from outside by other non-conformists like Georg Lukacs (1971), A. Gramsci (1971) and even from professional sociologists such as Norman Birnbaum and Tom Bottomore (see Birnbaum, 1971) who claimed to be Marxists themselves. Today, Marxism or Marxist social thought has hardly remained a homogeneous and unified system of ideas, of analysis and praxis (Bottomore, 1975: 65-75). As Immanuel Walterstein (1986: 1295-1308) has put it: 'Marxist era of Marx himself (1840s to 1883), the era of orthodox Marxism (from 1880s to about 1950) and then the era of 'thousand Marxisms' (since 1950s) are the three phases in which styles of utopia, rhetoric, and analytical rigours have undergone changes substantially. These changes, far from being accidental, were linked to social movements that were products of larger historical processes which were bound to bring about corresponding changes in the notion of relevance and praxis even within Marxist sociology.

The problem of relevance in Indian sociology

Much has been written on the growth of Indian sociology, its stages of development, and major influences in terms of theoretical, methodological and ideological orientations on the dominant trends in sociology in India since the 1920s (Mukherjee, 1979; Yogendra Singh, 1984a, 1986; Srinivas and Panini, 1973; Lele, 1981; Dhanagare, 1984). It is needless to go over their details as a hackneyed ritual once again in this paper. Nonetheless, it is necessary to tie them down to the entire question of relevance of sociology or relevant sociology in contemporary situation.

Indian sociologists have from time to time shifted their professional concerns and have redefined the relevance of what they did in response to changing historical forces. Studies on microcosms of social realities, such as caste, kinship, structures, marriage and family, village social structure and factional politics in village *panchayats*, and studies on tribal societies—the transition and social transformation they were going through—attracted considerable attention of professional sociologists in India till almost the mid-1960s. Macro-level processes of change set forth by colonialism, as well as by anti-imperialist national movement and by the forces of modernization—introduction of new education, an entirely new production technology and attendant value-structures also came to be studied. The problems of modern industrial society, such as poverty, slums, urban conglomerations, crime and deviance and industrial unrest as well as of youth identity and unrest also attracted considerable attention of researchers. The weaker and underprivileged sections, whether the scheduled castes, tribes, backward classes and women and their problems began to be focussed more sharply as gaps in developmental theory and practice were identified and plugged. Current interests in Indian sociology revolve around some of the neglected issues and questions in agrarian sociology, social movements, particularly protest movements, role of professions and, of course, the broader questions raised by development experience and its inextricable links with the core-periphery and dependency questions in the development debate itself.[4]

The changing ideas of relevance have thus kept pace with historical forces and this pace has been accelerated rather strikingly since the late 1960s or early 1970s. Indian sociology is neither any longer wallowing in complacency as it appeared to be where it was obsessed with micro-level social structures (Dhanagare, 1980), nor is it oblivious any longer to theoretical approaches or paradigms which came to be used, though only metaphorically rather than substantively by Indian sociologists (Singh, 1984a). Ideas of sociological intervention in social process are being offered increasingly as an alternative to the positivist paradigm, and its limitations are being increasingly highlighted.

If the industry was the epitome of the production of commodities and profit in the capitalist societies, production of theoretical and applied knowledge is the focal point of post-industrial societies. As Daniel Bell (1974: 26-27) and A. Touraine (1984) have pointed out, this production of knowledge takes place in universities and research organizations which have now come to occupy major positions in decision-making, planning policy formulation and hence in the power structures. Whether Indian society has completed the transition from pre-capitalist to capitalist or even to post-capitalist stages of development may still be an unsettled polemical issue. However, there is no denying the fact that Indian social sciences, at the institutional and intellectual levels, have developed a stature of their own by producing data bases as a result of their empirical inquiries. Policy implications of these were quickly grasped by those who were and are associated with policy planning, formulations and implementation.

Increasing demands on the craft of sociology are now being made by the state and its agencies and, to a certain extent, by private or corporate industrial business houses who also happen to be both the consumers of social science research and its principal promoters. Research priorities are identified by the state-sponsored funding agencies and business houses and the lines of inquiry are often laid down by them. Influx of research funds for foreign/international agencies also takes its own toll. The question of what is relevant sociology thus comes to be settled unilaterally either by the state or by the funding agencies. Under their impact sociology is rendered almost like a servicing-station, and this role is more often accepted passively by grant-seekers than it is examined critically.

Besides the state and big business and formal organizations, there are other, more silent, consumers of sociological knowledge. These consist of voluntary organizations, non-governmental, non-party action groups and activists as well as reformist-philanthropic bodies who want their strategic social interventions to be preceded by bench-mark surveys and analyses. If the present experience is any reckoner then it is clear that these organizations or groups engaged in amelioration, conscientization and mobilization of masses are going to make increasing demands on professional sociologists, and thereby redefine relevance of sociology in the years to come.

Two more determinants of relevance need to be mentioned. First, the canons of empirical sociology, following the dictates of the nineteenth century positivism, permeate and mainstream Indian sociology even today. Those in this stream still believe in the possibility of an objective, scientific and a value-neutral sociology.

Any social analyst's hobnobbing with social action, activism or with direct intervention evokes disapproval as irrelevant and unprofessional indulgence. In the mainstream framework of relevance the separation between 'analysis' and 'action' is steadfastly maintained. Any attempt to combine the two evokes sharp reaction. On the other side, as mentioned above, there are growing pressures from non-party action groups, voluntary NGOs or agencies to produce more relevant sociology in which analysis would be an effective instrument for praxis and for changing the micro-level scenarios in which these activist-groups functions.

To these growing pressures from the state, national and international agencies, business organizations as well as from action groups, reactions of professional sociologists tend to take three different forms: (a) complete submission and an uncritical acceptance (of grants, and hence of research priorites, theoretical approaches and conceptual categories), (b) rhetorical pleas for indigenisation of sociology, and (c) a total nihilistic dismissal of all posivitistic-empirical sociology. These three attitudes reflect either self-denial of sociology, a sulking and stultifying redundancy and anti-intellectualism—all of which are detrimental to the growth of a relevant sociology in any sense. Positivist ethos manifested in empirical inquiries is as useful as critical sociology and social criticism are. But then neither empiricist obsession nor hypercriticality can be conductive to counter-productive. Relevance and priorities, as defined by the state or private funding agencies, need not be outrightly rejected but then the sociological imagination must not be either mortagaged or sold out to the fund-suppliers or political activists, or non-party action groups. The real challenge for Indian sociologists lies not just in keeping all the channels of dialogue or expression open, but in combining and synthesizing the spirit of scientific inquiry, with social criticism—a role they can ill-afford to dispense with. The real problem is how do we produce a discourse with the state on the one hand and activists and masses on the other without losing or compromising our own autonomy in defining the relevance of what we do.

The synthesis of scientific spirit and social criticism, which we have advocated above, presupposes that in the ultimate analysis the question of 'relevance' cannot be settled purely in the arena of 'science' as such. It is quintessentially a 'value' question, a moral question and as such a matter of praxis—only determinate one as such because it is only when the nature of these values is utilitarian than 'science' (its positivist canons and spirit) could mediate. On the 'basic' moral question praxis would have to be guided by blind intuition or what is often called the 'voice of conscience'[5]. In this sense the issue of relevance as well as accountability of sociology would always be settled in the minds of analysts, i.e., practitioners of sociology.

Notes

1. Some of these have been discussed by Peter Berger (1963).
2. To Gouldner, the historical mission of 'reflexive sociology' is to transcend sociology as it now exists and in order to succeed in this mission, it will have to be more radical. For details, see Gouldner (1970: 488-500).
3. To cite an example, this kind of functionalist orientation is evident in Blau and Scott's treatment of formal organization. See Blau and Scott (1962).
4. At least some of these thematic thrusts, and the research done on them by Indian sociologists and social anthropologists have been reviewed in the two series of Trend Reports published by the ICSSR covering the period up to 1979.
5. This formulation is based on written comments of Prof. Yogendra Singh on my paper, and which he conveyed to the author through a personal communication.

References

Apter, David E. (Ed.), 1964. *Ideology and Discontent* (with Introduction by Apter himself), New York: Free Press, pp. 15-46.

Bell, Daniel, 1974. *The Coming of Post-industrial Society:A Venture in Social Forecasting*, New York: Basic Books.

Berger, Peter L., 1963. *Invitation to Sociology:A Humanistic Perspective*,

New York: Anchor Books/Doubleday and Co.

Blau, Peter M. and Scott, W.R., 1962. *Formal Organizations:A Comparative Approach*, San Francisco: Chandeler Publisher.

Birnbaum, Norman, 1971. *Towards a Critical Sociology*, New York: Oxford University Press, pp. 94-129.

Bottomore T., 1969. *Critics of Society:Radical Thought in North America*, London: George Allen and Unwin.

1974. *Sociology as Social Criticism*, New York: Pantheon Books.

1975. *Marxist Sociology* (Studies in Sociology Series), London: Mac millan.

1984, *The Frankfurt School*, London: George Allen and Unwin.

Collins, Randall, 1986. "Is 1980s Sociology in the Doldrums", *American Journal of Sociology*, Vol. 91, No. 6 (May 1986), pp. 1336-55.

Dhanagare D.N., 1980, "Search for Identity", *Seminar*, No. 254 (October 1980), pp. 23-26.

1984, "Sociology and Social Anthropology—India", in Y. Atal (Ed.), *Sociology and Social Anthropology in Asian and the Pacific*, Paris: UNESCO/Wiley India.

Freund, J., 1972. *The Sociology of Max Weber*, Harmondsworth: Penguin Books.

Gouldner, A.W., 1970. *The Coming Crisis of Western Sociology*, New York: Basic Books.

Gramsci, A., 1971. *Selections from the Prison Notebooks*, London: Lawrence and Wishart.

Hempel, C. and Oppenheim P., 1948. 'The Logic of Explanation', *Philosophy of Science*, Vol. 15, pp. 125-75.

Kaplan, A., 1964. *The Conduct of Inquiry:Methodology for Behavioural Science*, San Francisco: Chandler Publishing Co.

Lele, J., 1981. "Indian Sociology and Sociology in India: Some Reflexions on their Being", *Sociological Bulletin*, Vol. 30 No. 1 (March), pp. 39-53.

Lukacs, Georg, 1971. *History and Class Consciousness*, London: Merlin Press.

Marx, K., 1970. *The Critique of Hegel's Phiolosophy of Right* (with an introduction by O. Malley), Cambridge University Press.

Mills, C. Wright, 1962. *Power Politics and People* (The collected essays of C. Wright Mills edited and with an introduction by Irving Herewitz), New York: Ballantine Books.

Mukherjee, R., 1979. *Sociology of Indian Sociology*, Bombay: Allied.

Parsons, T., 1970. *The Social System*, London: Routledge and Kegan Paul.

Rex, J. (Eds.), 1974. *Approaches to Sociology: An Introduction to Major Trends in British Sociology*, London: Routledge & Kegan Paul.

Saran, A.K., 1962. 'Some Aspects of Positivism in Sociology', *Transactions of the Fifth World Congress of Sociology*, Vol. I (International Sociology Association), pp. 199-233.

Sayer, Derek, 1983. *Marx's Method:Ideology, Science and Critique in 'Capital'*, Brighton, Sussex: The Harvester Press (particularly Chapter 5, 'To bring a science by criticism', pp. 105-41).

Srinivas, M.N. and Panini, M.N., 1973. 'The development of sociology and social anthropology in India', *Sociological Bulletin*, Vol. 22 No. 2 (September), pp. 179-215.

Singh, Y., 1984a. *Image of Man:Theory and Ideology in Indian Sociology*, Delhi: Chanakya Publications.

1984b, 'Relevant Sociology—Part-I, Conceptual Issues, Part-II Indian Situation', *Relevant Sociology*, Vol. I Nos. 1-2, pp. 5-17; 3-13.

1986. *Indian Sociology:Social Conditioning and Emerging Concerns*, New Delhi: Vistar Publications.

Touraine, A., 1984. 'The Waning of Sociological Image of Social Life', *International Journal of Comparative Sociology*, Vol. XXV, Nos. 1-2, pp. 33-44.

Wallerstein, I., 1986. 'Marxisms as Utopias: Evolving Ideologies', *American Journal of Sociology*, Vol. 91, No. 6 (May 1986), pp. 1295-1308.

Author index

Subject index